Edmund Ignatius Hogan

Irish Phrase Book

illustrating the various meanings and uses of verbs and prepositions combined

Edmund Ignatius Hogan

Irish Phrase Book
illustrating the various meanings and uses of verbs and prepositions combined

ISBN/EAN: 9783337734510

Printed in Europe, USA, Canada, Australia, Japan

Cover: Foto ©Andreas Hilbeck / pixelio.de

More available books at **www.hansebooks.com**

IRISH PHRASE BOOK,

ILLUSTRATING

THE VARIOUS MEANINGS AND USES

OF

VERBS AND PREPOSITIONS

COMBINED.

BY

The Rev. EDMUND HOGAN, s.j., m.r.i.a.,

CELTIC EXAMINER, R.U.I.; AND ROYAL IRISH ACADEMY'S
TODD PROFESSOR OF THE CELTIC LANGUAGES.

DUBLIN:

SULLIVAN, BROTHERS
(A. THOM & CO., Limited),
26 and 27 MARLBOROUGH STREET,

1899.

INTRODUCTION.

In English the direct object of a verb is in the accusative case, and all other cases attached to verbs are considered as indirect objects. But not unfrequently in Latin and other languages the indirect object (in the genitive, dative, ablative, or prepositional case), corresponds to the direct object in English, as 'placuit mihi,' it pleased me; 'parce populo,' spare the people; 'nuire à la santé,' to injure the health; 'ich danke Ihnen,' I thank you; 'er folgt mir' or 'er folgt auf mich,' he follows me. So in Irish the indirect or prepositional cases are often used where the English have the accusative, as, 'beir air,' catch him; 'gab air,' beat him; 'altuiġim lé Dia,' I thank God. This indirect object, following verbs after the manner of the English direct object, is adequately dealt with in all grammars and dictionaries except the Irish. Even the prepositional cases are fully treated, and the importance of prepositions in human speech finds due recognition from all, save perhaps our Irish grammarians, who treat these important little particles with unmerited neglect. One hundred pages of Mr. Roby's Latin Syntax, one-fourth of Dr. Abbott's "Latin Prose through English Idiom," one-sixth of Dr. Joyce's Grammar, are devoted to them.

To the elucidation of their meanings and uses are given twenty pages, and these the best and most original of O'Donovan's Grammar. His reasons for dwelling so much on that subject were : 1. Lest the meanings should become almost unintelligible, if the language ceased to be a spoken language ; 2. Because the idiomatic meanings are not fully[1] indicated in any Irish dictionary, and present *almost insuperable* difficulties to such as attempt the study of the language.

Yet, notwithstanding these almost insuperable difficulties, O'Donovan says at p. 84 : " Some verbs require a preposition, as *iarr ar Dhia*, ask of God, *labhair lé Domnall*, speak to Daniel; but these forms must be learned by experience in this as in all other languages." O'Donovan's excuse for neglecting this essential part of Irish syntax has no foundation in fact, since the grammars and dictionaries of ' other languages ' such as Greek, Latin, German and French, contain all, or most of the information required on this matter ; while, alas ! the Irish student is condemned to pick it up by ' experience,' Yet in Irish the prepositions are 33, or 50, or 66 per cent more in use than in the aforesaid languages ; and besides, in Irish more than in those tongues the verb and preposition blend in a peculiar manner, and impart to each other and to their combination a fresh force and significance. This I will endeavour to show by some statistics and examples :—

1. Ten passages, taken almost at random, from various parts of the Irish Bible, contain 3,000 words, of which 508 are prepositions ; while the corresponding texts of five other versions contain only 323 English, 304 French, 236 German, 158 Latin, and 140 Greek prepositions. Hence it seems specially necessary to know the various and peculiar functions of these little Irish particles, which play so large and lively a part in Irish speech as to form one-sixth of Irish literature and conversation.

2. Our book will show how verbs and prepositions, when combined, acquire a new significance. I here give only a few instances. *Rug mé ar fheusbig air* of the Irish Bible, 1 Samuel xvii., 35, is literally, ' I bore on beard on him ' ; but it means in

---

[1] O'Donovan's Grammar, p. 290 ; he should have said that the idiomatic meanings are not indicated at all.

English, 'I caught him by his beard ;' in German 'ich fasste ihn beim bart;' in French, 'je le pris par la barbe,' in the Latin Bible, 'apprehendebam barbam ejus.' No Middle Grade boy, who knows the signification of each word of 'the other languages,' would miss the meaning of the whole; whereas the pupils of the same grade, guided 'by experience,' gave me twenty-five different, and incorrect and amusing versions of that phrase of four words.[1] They could get no light from dictionaries and grammars, though they might have guessed the meaning from the context or from Dr. Joyce's 'Idiom 24,' *rug orra*, 'he overtook them.'

Even ripe scholars do not 'learn by experience' all about these Irish idiomatic combinations. To say nothing of Continental Celtologists, who have not lived in an Irish atmosphere, Dr. Atkinson, who is widely and deeply read in Irish literature sometimes misunderstands a phrase, though he understands every word thereof. For example, in his admirable edition of Keating's 'Three Shafts of Death,' he twice, at pp. 359, 381, mistranslates *géabthar air* of p. 96. He renders it; 'it shall be behaved to him, he shall be treate l.' The context shows that it means 'he shall be *mal*treated ;' and further, that it signifies 'he shall be beaten,' as the text refers to St. Luke, xii. 47, where *géabhthar móráu air* (of the Irish Bible) is 'he shall be beaten with many stripes,' in the English version. Many instances of this not uncommon idiom are given in our Phrase-Book.

Again, who has learned more Irish 'by experience,' who has read, written and printed more than Mr. Whitley Stokes? Yet he is puzzled in presence of an old Irish gloss in which this idiom occurs, and says, 'In this gloss, both Latin and Irish are obscure to me.'[2] I will attempt a translation, which I hope may meet with his approval. St. Paul asks the Corinthians: "Where

---

is the wise? where is the disputer of this world? Hath not God made foolish the wisdom of this world?" Of course the answer is, that the wise, the disputer of the world is nowhere; and the Glossarist of the eighth or ninth century remarks, partly in Latin, partly in Irish: "Where shall appear a wise gentile of the Greeks? it is a question which he asked" (that is the question); "for one school attacks or beats the other." The meaning is "Where are the wise men?" Echo answers, 'Where?' They are nowhere, since one set of philosophers calls the others fools, and proclaims that their 'wisdom' is what Horace calls *insaniens sapientia*. The gloss runs runs thus: "(Ubi sapiens) apparebit gentiles (*read* gentilis) de Graecis .i. bid cuingid rochuingid ar gebaid (ó)in scol for aléli;" gebaid for = "goes for," of the Americans.

My translation seems vouched for by *géabthar air*, etc., previously quoted, and by phrases which are printed in this book. Many distinguished Celtologists of the Continent have been bewildered by the idiomatic use of prepositions with verbs, and, finding no light from Zeuss or O'Donovan, they either mistranslate the text or declare it to be defective or corrupt. But as this is not the place for a full discussion of such matters, I will end with an example of mistranslation by Dr. Geisler, a German Professor of Galway College, whose ardent pursuit of Irish studies has been interrupted by death. In his "Irish Texts," 1st Series, Part I., p. 14, *Ní do áitrebtadib in betha frecnairc dúinne*, is wrongly rendered, 'we do not attach ourselves to the inhabitants of the present world,' whereas the meaning is 'we are not of the inhabitants of the present world.' This is a common Irish idiom, as *do Chorco Oche don Chumull sin*, 'of the Corco Oche that Cumall was', "Mac-ġníomartha Fhinn," 10; *do Chorca Laoiġde d'Fhearadach*, Fearadach was of the Corca Laoiġde, 'Fragments of Irish Annals,' p. 8.

When mature scholars find themselves at fault in these matters, what must it be with Irish boys, who are so inadequately equipped with texts, dictionaries and grammars? Since, then, the prepositions present 'almost insuperable difficulties' in Irish, and figure 33, 50, or 66 per cent more frequently, and affect and modify the meanings of verbs more profoundly than in English, French, German, Latin, or Greek, they demand more attention and fuller treatment than have hitherto been bestowed upon them.

If translators had more acquaintance with Irish idiom, they would not have rendered *tuccus* (*seirc, grád, díograis*) *duit* by "I have directed my love to thee," "I have shown love to thee," "I have bestowed love upon thee." To an Irish speaker these words mean this and nothing more: "I have loved you," as may be seen at the word "love" in the dictionaries of O'Begley and Foley. So in Donlevy, pp. 490, 55, "*do thabhairt grádh d'á chomharsain, grádh ar g-croídhe go hiomlán do thabhairt Dó*" means "to love his neighbour, to love Him with our whole heart." Attention to this will save us from being overwhelmed by the following declaration of love which we meet with in translations:—"I have directed my love to thee on the ground of the great tidings of thee"—"c'est magnifique, mais ce n'est pas l'amour," and I venture to think that neither our grannies nor our Gráinnes ever spoke in that sublime fashion.

Our Phrase-Book is an attempt to supply a great want. In it are given more than two hundred verbs, which, in combination with the preposition *ar*, present generally an idiomatic meaning, and illustrate an important and hitherto neglected part of the syntax of verbs and prepositions. While keeping that object always in view, I exemplify the uses of other verbs and prepositions, and introduce as much variety as possible, in order to give help towards the study of texts, and the preparation for composition in the different grades of Primary, Intermediate and University Examinations. The Irish sentences and English versions are those of Irishmen who spoke and wrote both languages ; and to their books sufficient reference is given, but in such a way as not to crowd the pages and distract the reader.

As to Irish type, 1°, it is beautiful to look at, though like the German and Greek it is more trying to the sight than the Roman ; 2°, its d, f and t bear the dots with more grace than does the Roman ; 3°, it is our own Irish character, and should be as patriotically preserved as are the German and Greek ; 4°, though many Germans and others fancy that the Teutons would show their sense and spare their eyesight by adopting the Roman type, a people so highly conservative as the Irish ought to cling to their characters at all costs, and shrink from imitating their canny kinsfolk of Scotland.

As an Irishman I could not but feel the force and weight of all this ; and I fancy that it might be well to publish in Irish text the books of learned societies, when they have plenty of money and their writers have plenty of time. But I deem it useful and patriotic not to employ Irish letters in elementary books, for the following reasons combined :—1°. They are the old Roman, which Rome, and the world, except Ireland, have discarded for the improved modern Roman. 2°. They are the type which Queen Elizabeth was the first to get cast, in order to win the Irish from " Romanism " ; she failed in that intent, but struck at the Irish language and literature a blow under which it has reeled for three centuries. 3°. To write in Irish letters costs 20 or 30 per cent. more of valuable time, and thus prevents people from preparing more texts and translations to supply the wants of Irish students. 4°. Irish type costs purchasers and writers 33 per cent. more money, since in Ireland ' Irish ' printing costs the same as Greek or German. 5°. In setting up, and afterwards in correcting, Irish type, so many mistakes are made, that authors are condemned to loss of time, temper, and money, and to see their published books teeming with typographical errors. 6°. The Irish or old Roman type is not supplemented by italics or their equivalent, and italics are absolutely necessary for a correct and scholarly presentment of Irish texts. 7°. As teacher and examiner, I know that boys in learning to write, and in writing, Irish text, lose half or one-third of their time, which would be better spent in learning the language and literature of Ireland. 8°. In the compositions of the boys of the Intermediate grades, I have met with an almost peerless specimen of Irish penmanship, and it was the work of a lad who knew almost nothing of Irish ; but as a rule, the writing was so wretched as almost to deter a person from reading it. Hence, I am sure that while the students will find more ease in writing their compositions and exercises in Roman hand, the numerous teachers throughout the country will find more comfort in reading and correcting them. 9°. Many gifted Irishmen and Scots who speak Gaelic from their childhood, and are saturated with it, have been and are deterred from reading Irish books by the strange look of the letters, and fancy it is a language unknown to them. 10°. Since I feel that for these reasons Irish type is not as good as the modern Roman, I do not employ it, as I would not use an old Roman or Irish plough, or go in a boat, like St. Brendan's, from Kingstown to Holyhead, or in a 'chariot' like Cuchulaind's from Dublin to Cork ; or give up coal, gas and the electric light for turf, rush lights and candles.

In books the nine aspirated consonants are marked with dots, or with h's (as in O'Brien's Dictionary) ; so that the pages are crowded with dots or h's. By printing ph, ch and th, as they are written in old Irish, I diminish the dots by one-third or more, and lessen the proverbial danger of omitting the dots ; by dotting the other six letters I diminish the h's by about one-third. I propose this compromise to the partisans of both methods of aspiration ; and I even think it would be well, though I do not venture so far, to confine the dot, or *punctum delens*, to the silent consonants, as that would be a good guide to pronunciation, and as the dot was originally used to mark the suppression of the form or sound of a letter. Again as the accents and a's are innumerable in Irish, after the example of good writers[1] I cut them down considerably by writing *eu* for *éa*, and diminish the danger of omitting the accent over *é*. Thus *fér* of old Irish, becomes *féar, féur*, and better *feur*, as *eu* is equal to *éa* in sound.

As to the forms of the tenses of the verbs, I follow the good authorities, which I here append with the marks of abbreviation:

A.   Acts of the Apostles, ed. 1602.

a.   Ancient Irish.

b.   O'Begley's English-Irish Dictionary, ed. 1732.

d.   Donlevy's Irish-English Catechism, ed. 1745.

dg.   Diarmaid and Grainne, ed. by Mr. O'Grady.

ex.   Book of Exodus, 1681.

fa.   Fragments of Irish Annals, ed. 1860.

j.   Gospel of St. John, 1602.

k.   Keating's Hist. of Ireland, ed. by Haliday.

L.   Children of Lir.   Second Edition.

l.   Gospel of St. Luke, ed. 1595-1602.

m.   Gospel of St. Matthew, 1595.

mk.   Gospel of St. Mark, 1595.

o.   Other preposition or verb used.

ob.   O'Brien's Irish-English Dictionary, 1768

od.   O'Donovan's Grammar.

ps.   Psalms, 1681.

pr.   Book of Proverbs, 1681.

s.   Three Shafts of Death by Keating, ed. by Dr. Atkinson.

While this Phrase-Book may furnish comparative philologists and advanced students with some matter for reflection, it is meant chiefly for beginners ; and hence it presents two or three hundred verbs in various moods and tenses, not only in conjunction with prepositional phrases, but with a great number of useful words.

---

[1] As Gearnon in his "Parrthas an Anma," edited 1645.

VERBS AND PREPOSITIONS.

Verbs followed by the preposition **ar, on,** old Irish **for.**

Beirim, I bear.

1. rug mé ar ḟeusóig air.

I caught him by the beard,
    1 *Sam.* 18.

do breith ar an uain ar úrlad.

to take occasion by the fore-lock,   *b.* 507.

ar m-breith dóib-sion ar laiṁ air do threoruiġeadar go Damascus é.

taking him by the hand they led him to Damascus,
    Acts. 9.

rug sé ar láiṁ uirre agus do éiriġ an cailín.

he took her by the hand and the maid arose,
    m. 9, *mk.* 5, *l.* 8.

beiris ar chluasaiḃ air.

he caught him by the ears,
    s. 207.

ar m-breiṫ ar an arán ; beiriḋ an spiorad air ; ar m-breith air.

taking the bread ; the spirit taketh him ; laying hold of him,   *l.* 24, 9.

gíod bé neach d'á d-tiubra misi póg, as é sin é, beiriḋ air ; an tráṫ do ṡanluiġeadar breith air, do bí eagla an phobuil orra ; ar m-breiṫ ar Iosa dóib-sean.

whomsoever I shall kiss, that same is he, hold him fast ; when they sought to take him they feared the people ; laying hold of Jesus,
    m. 26, 21, 26.

má's gasta an geirr-ḟiad beirthear fá deiread air

if the hare is swift, it is caught at last,   *Proverb.*

cia agaiḃ si duine nach beurad uirre agus nach d-tóigeabad aníos í ?

what man among you would not lay hold of her and lift her up ?   *m.* 12

ní rugabar orm ; rugadar ar a chosaib-sion.

ye laid no hold on me; they held him by the feet,
m. 26, 28.

beirid air agus tabraid lib ; cionnas do beuraidís a b-feill air-sion ; rugadar na hógánaig air.

take and lead him away ; how they might take him by craft ; the young men laid hold of him. *mk.* 14, 15, 14.

ar m-breíth do Pheadar air do thionnsgain achmusán do thabairt dó.

Peter took and began to rebuke him, *mk.* 8.

rugadar na sgológa orra, agus do gabadar ar fear díob agus do gabadar do chlochaib ar fear eile.

the husbandmen took them, and beat one and stoned another, *m.* 21.

ag sínead a láime ar an m-ball d'Iosa, rug sé air.

Jesus immediately stretched forth his hand and caught him, *mk.* 14.

ann sin rug Diarmaid ar Ghráinne

then Diarmaid caught Gráinne *dg.* 146.

do breith ar dreangcuid.

to catch a flea. *b.* 221.

má beirthear é aiseocaid sé seacht n-oirid.

if he be caught, he shall restore sevenfold, *pr.* 6.

ar m-breith ar leanb dó do chuir sé ann a lár é.

he took a child and set him in the midst of them. *mk.* 9.

beirim ort, *Lucerna Fidel.* 338

I hold you, I have you.

do breith air a m-bréig folluis.

to take him in a flat lie. *b.* 220.

do rugad orm go cealgach.

I brought my hogs to a fine market, *b.* 316.

do rugad air.

he was taken, *ob* 409.

do breith air san n-gníom ;

to catch him in the act, *b.* 107.

má beirir ar muic, beir ar chois uirre.

if you catch a pig catch it by the foot, *b.* 375.

gach uile ball a m-beireann sé é, tairngid sé as a chéile é.

wheresoever he taketh him he teareth him, *mk.* 9.

an té chuimleas re ceannairg nach baineann ris, is cosmuil é ré neach beireas ar mhadrad ar a chluasaib.

he that meddles with strife not belonging to him, is like one that takes a dog by the ears, *pr.* 26.

ag cur chuige rugadar air agus tugadar leo.

they came upon him and caught him and took him,
Acts, 6

rug sé ar an laoġ noch do rinneadar, agus do ṁeill sé 'na luaithread é, agus do leathnuiġ ar an uisge é, agus tug ar chloin Israel d'ól de.

he took the call which they made and ground it into powder, and strewed it on the water, and made the children of Israel drink it.
ex. 32.

do breith ar siúbal.

to bring away,   *b.* 89.

do breith go cruaid ar ní.

to grasp a thing,   *b.* 273.

a breith air laiṁ oirre d'éiġ é, ' a chaileag eirich !'

taking her by the hand he called, ' Maid, arise,'
l. 8, *Scotch Bible.*

2. beuraid an t-oireaṁ ar an m-buainaiġe ; do rug sé orra.

the ploughman will overtake the reaper ; he overtook them.   *ob.* 481, 409.

ro arraid orra. 1. ruc orra.

rug sé orra ag Sulchóid ; fanfad-sa leat ar an láthair so nó go m-beirir ormsa arís ; fágbam an tulach so d'eagla go m-beurad A. orrainn.

he overtook them at Sulchoid ; I will wait for you at this place till you overtake me again ; let us leave this hill for fear that A. should overtake us,   *dg.* 194.

beirit clann Doṁnaill orra.

Donall's sons overtake them,
4 *Mast.* 1541.

do rug an teasbach mór orra,

they were overtaken by the great heat,   *dg.* 142.

ní rugad uirre ; rug oidche orro.

she was not overtaken ; night overtook them. *L.* 64, 43.

cuirid tóruiġeacht orra go luath, óir beurthaoi orra.

give them chase quickly, for ye shall overtake them,
Joshua 20.

creud a luas do rugad ort !

how soon you were overtaken !
b. 327.

is minic do rug fear an deich ar fear an dá fichid.

often has the man of the ten overtaken the man of the twenty,   *Prov.*

3. creud é an duine as a m-beireann tú aithne air ?

what is man that thou hast respect unto him ?   *ps.* 144.

ní rugamar an báire ar a chéile.

we did not win the goal against one another, *dg.* 118.

as sin thiocfas do breith breithe ar beoaib agus ar ṁarbuib.

thence He shall come to judge the living and the dead,
Creed.

beuraid siad breith báis air.

ná beirid breath dochum nach
beurthaoi breath orruib ;
óir is do réir na breithe
beirthi beurthar breath
orruib-si.

an tan beirthear breitheamnas
ort,

beurthar breitheamnas fá leith
ort.

atáim am' seasam ag cathaoir
breitheamnuis Shéasair, ann
ar cóir breath do breith orm.

beuraid an Tigearna breitheamnas ar an b-pobal.

tugadar na hárdsagairt é chum
breitheamnais (nó chum
breithe báis) do breith air.

4. ro innis sé nár b-féidir le
neart buaid do breith air,
muna m-beurfaddraoideacht
air.

is air is déideanuige do beir-
mid buaid.

rug sé buaid ar a náimdib.

is í so an buaid rug buaid ar an
t-saogal.

beirid sé buaid air.

adeirim-se riot nach beuraid
geatuide ifeirn buaid uirthe.

an tan nach deunann sé dúthracht chum buada do breith
ar a lochtaib.

o. iar m-breith buada ó doman
agus ó deaman.

ao. rucc A. cosgair iomda do
Laignib.

they shall condemn him to
death,   *mk.* 10, *m.* 20.

judge not that ye be not
judged ; for with what judgment ye judge ye shall be
judged,   *m.* 7, *l.* 6.

when thou art judged.

you shall undergo a particular
judgment,   *d.* 186.

I stand at Cæsar's judgment
seat, where I ought to be
judged,   *A.* 25.

the Lord shall judge the
people,   *ps.* 7.

the high priests delivered him
to be condemned to death,
l. 24.

he told that it is not possible
by force to vanquish him,
unless magic should take
hold of him,   *dg.* 166.

it is the last one we overcome,
d. 156.

he conquered his enemies,
d. 402.

this is the victory that overcame the world,   1 *John,* 5.

he overcomes him,   *l.* 11.

I say unto thee, that the gates
of hell shall not prevail
against her.   *m.* 16.

when he uses no diligence to
overcome his failings, *d.* 174.
cfr. John 5.

after having gained a victory
over the world and the
demon,   4 *Mast.* 1616.

A. gained many victories over
Leinstermen.   *fa.* 12.

rugadar buaid orm.

céim do breith ar Chonal.
5. beir sé éigean ar bochtaib.
iarraid sé air í féin do breith
ar élod ó Chonchúbar.
d'á faide a's beideas tú amach
na beir droichsgeul a baile
ort féin.
ní b-fuil mac ríg nár rug
m'ingion-sa eurad tochmaire
air.

beirid a coiscéime greim ar
ifrionn.
o. glac greim daingion do
theagasg, is crann beatha é
don druing glacas greim de.
rugadar leo é ar maluide an
t-sléibe.
má beir sé sathad air.

atá sé ag teacht chum tuigsean-
ad do breith ar a beartaib
féin.
beuraid aon madrad amháin ar
madraide an baile tafann.
ná léig d'urchóid ar bith uach-
taránacht do breith orm.

they have prevailed against
me, *ps*. 129.
to outdo, outstrip Conal, *k*. lii.
he doth ravish the poor, *ps*. 10.
she asks him to elope with
her from Conor, *k*. 370.
as long as you are away don't
bring home a bad story
about yourself, *Proverb*.
there is no son of a king to
whom my daughter has not
given a refusal of marriage,
dg. 44.
her steps take hold of hell,
pr. 5.
take fast hold of instruction,
it is a tree of life to them that
lay hold on her, *pr*. 4. 3.
they led him unto the brow of
the hill, *l*. 4.
if he makes a thrust at him,
ob. 418.
he begins already to know
himself, *b*. 387.

one single dog will set all the
dogs of the village barking.
let no wickedness have do-
minion over me, *ps*. 119.

Dobeirim, I give. *O.I.* dobiur.

1. dobeurair orm gáirdeachas
do chlos.
dobeuraid mé ar iasg h-ainimib
seasam ar do lannaib.

thugais ar an d-talam crioth-
nugad.
dobeurad ar mo múitheas uile
dul rómad.

thou shalt make me hear of
joy, *ps*. 51.
I will cause the fish of your
rivers to stick to your scales,
ob. 316.
thou hast made the land to
shake, *ps*. 60.
I will make all my goodness
pass before thee, *ex*. 33.

subáilce dobeir orruinn a chuid féin do thabairt do gach aon.
a virtue which makes us render his due to everyone, *d.* 198.

an uair thaitnid slíġthe an duine leis an Tiġearna, dobeir sé ar a námaid féin beith síodach ris.
when the ways of a man please the Lord, he makes even his enemies to be at peace with him, *pr.* 16.

thug tú ar daoinib marcuiġeacht do deunaṁ ar ár g-ceannaib.
thou has caused men to ride over our heads, *ps.* 66.

an bean thug ort a labairt.
the woman who induced you to speak, *L.* 69.

an b-feudtaoi-si a thabairt ar chloinn seomra an fir nuaphósda trosgad do deunad?
can ye make the children of the bride-chamber fast? *l.* 5.

do thabairt ar an lóchrann lasad a g cóṁnuide.
to cause the lamp to burn always, *ex.* 27.

tug tú orm dóthchus do beith orm agus mé ar chíochaib mo ṁáthar.
thou madest me to hope when I was on my mother's breasts, *ps.* 22.

gnáthuġad na n-guasacht dobeir orruinn a n-díṁeasad.
the familiarity of dangers brings us to contemn them, *b.* 89.

do thugamar ar an b-fear so siúbal.
we have made this man walk, *A.* 3.

do thug sé ar gach uile chrann fás.
he makes every tree to grow, *ob.* 94.

thug sé orm cóṁnuide do deunaṁ a n-dorchadus.
he made me to dwell in darkness, *ps.* 143.

dobeir sé orm luíge a n-inbear féir ṁinlig.
he causes me to lie in a pasture of fine grass, *ps.* 23.

dobeir an crannchair ar imreasánaib cosg.
the lot causes contentions to cease, *pr.* 18.

gid bé beireas ar an b-fíreun seachrán, tuitfid sé féin ion a pholl.
whoso causeth the righteous to go astray, he shall himself fall into his own pit, *pr.* 28.

dobeirir ar dul amach na maidne luathġáir do deunaṁ.
thou makest the outgoing of the morning to rejoice, *ps.* 65.

buideachas ar Dhia go d-tug mé ort fá deiread siar sin d'adṁáil.
thank God that I have made you at long last admit that, *Lucerna Fidel.* 317

thugais orrainn íon an mea-
ruigthe d'ól.
ag tabairt air labairt ar mórán
do néithib.
dobeir fós orra lingead amuil
laog.
tug ar chloinn Israel d'ól de.

dobeura tú orra ól d'aibnib
h-aoibnis

beirthear a g-codlad uatha
muna d-tugaid ar chuid
éigin tuitim.
tug air ingean Ui Raigillig do
léigean.
dobeir dóbrón a g-croide
duine air cromad, acht dogní
focal maith sólásach é.
thug ar an b-foirinn do chuaid
leis an chríoch sin d'áitiú-
gad.
atá spadántacht dobeir orruinn
gnóthuige Dé do leígean
dínn.
tabair ar th-fear go n-innscad
sé dúinne an tóihus.

o. creud dobeir ag deunad
moille thú?
tabair ar h-agaid lonnrúgad
orm agus teagaisg dam do
reachta.
dobeirir ar a sgéim cnaoi mar
leothan ag cnaoi cudaig.

tug C. ar Bh. deoch do thabairt ar Sg.
adeirim rib go d-tugann sé
uirre adaltrannas do deu-
nam.

thou hast made us drink of the
wine of confusion, *ps.* 60.
provoking him to speak of
many things, *l.* 11.
he makes them also to skip
like a calf, *ps.* 29.
he made the children of Israel
drink it, *ex.* 32.
thou wilt make them drink of
the rivers of thy delight,
ps. 36.
their sleep is taken away,
unless they cause some to
fall, *pr.* 4.
he induced him to put away
O'Reilly's daughter, *od.*
heaviness in the heart of man
maketh it stoop, but a good
word maketh it glad, *pr.* 13.
he caused the band that went
with him to inhabit that
territory, *k.* xiv.
it is a slackness, which makes
us omit the service of God,
d. 172.
entice your husband that he
may declare unto us the
riddle, *Judges* 14.
why tarriest thou? *J.* 22.

make thy face to shine on me
and teach me thy laws,
ps. 119.
thou makest his beauty to
consume away like as a moth
fretteth a garment, *ps.*
C. caused B. to give Sg. a
drink, *od*
I say unto you that he causeth
her to commit adultery,
m. 5.

dobeirid a n-anmanna féin ar a n-dúthaiġ.

they give their own names to their land, *ps.* 49.

lé mórán do chaint blasda thug sí air aontuġad.

with much fair speech she caused him to yield, *pr.* 7.

dobeir tú orrainn iompód ó n-ár nániuid.

thou makest us to turn our backs upon our enemies, *ps.* 44.

chor go d-tuga mé ar an n-droing lé'r b'ionmuin mé saidbrios do ṡealbúġad.

that I may cause them that love me to inherit wealth, *pr.* 8.

a. tucc se fá deara forru.

he commanded, obliged them, *ob.* 168.

go d-tugaid Dia fá deara ar a ġnúis deallrad ort.

may God make his countenance shine upon thee !

tugadar fa deara ar Bhretnaib cloide do deunaṁ do chaoṁnad na m-Bretan ar im-ruagad na n-Gaodal.

they compelled the Britons to make a fosse to protect the Britons against the incursion of the Irish, *k.* x.

o. dobeirid sé fá deara go g-cluinid na bodair.

he maketh the deaf to hear, *mk.* 7.

2. tabair aġaid orra.

face them, *od.*

ar d-tabairt aġaid don t-ṡagart ar an b-pobul.

the priest turning his face to the people.

mar tug-soṁ a aiġid forra.

as he turned towards them, *fa.* 172.

d'iarr sé orra aire do thabairt ar theagasg na b-Fairisí-neach ; dubairt mé rib bur n-aire do thabairt daoib ar laibín na b-Fairisíneach.

he bid them beware of the doctrine of the Pharisees ; I have told you to beware of the leaven of the Pharisees, *m.* 16.

tabair aire ar do chéimionnaib.

look to your hits, *b.* 315.

o. tugaid aire rib féin.

look to yourselves, *j.* 2*d. Epist.*

3. creud an t-ainm bá mian leis do thabairt air.

how he would have him called, *l.* 1.

ainm tugthar ar an diabal.

a name which is given to the devil, *b.* 162.

an cheud ainm tugad ar Eirinn.

the first name that was given to Ireland, *od.*

beuraid sí mac, agus dobeura tú Iosa d'ainm air ; tug sé Iosa d'ainm air.

she shall bring forth a son and thou shalt call his name Jesus ; he called his name Jesus, *m.* 1 ; *l.* 1.

dobeura tú Eoin mar ainm air.

daid, ainm beirid leinb óga ar a n-aithreacha, agus fós goirid 'pápá' díob.

cia an t-ainm dobeir tú air?
do thug sé leasanmnad orm.

Tadg O'Suilleabáin do thug an sagart orm.
dobeir sé clodaire orm.
creud í an urnaigde sin ar a d-tugair 'mídeamhuin'?
creud fá d-tugthar subáilcide bunadusacha orra?
mar go d-tug 'cleas' ar an g-cleas sin.
creud fá d-tugthar peacad air?
airmid sé uimir na reultan agus dobeir sé anmanna orra uile.

o. creud fá n-goirthear ceinn-pheacaide díob?
an greideal ag tabairt 'tón dub' ar an b-pota.
5 ro fiafruig Finn d'fiannaib Eirionn a d-tugadar aithne air.
go d-tiobraidís aithne orro,

aithne nó taithige do thabairt duit ar an ní sin
do thabairt ar aithne
tucsat an sluag aithne fair gur bé cenn Duinnbo.
thugus aithne air romhadsa,

d'aithin sé ormsa nachar b'amudán mé.
tug sé aithne uirri.

thou shalt call his name John,
l. 1.
daddy, a name which young children give their fathers, and they also call them papa, b. 149.
how do you name him?
he called me a nickname,
b. 484.
the priest christened me Teig O'Sullevan.
he calls me a rogue, b. 99.
what is that prayer which you call 'meditation?' d. 450.
why are they called cardinal virtues? d. 198.
as he called that feat 'a feat,'
dg. 84.
why is it called a sin? d. 152.
he telleth the number of the stars and calleth them all by their names, ps. 147.
why are they called capital sins? d. 154.
the griddle calling the pot 'black bottom,' Proverb.
Finn asked the fianna of Erin if they knew him, dg. 122.

that they might recognize them. L. 47.
to make you acquainted with that, s. 349.
to usher in, introduce, b. 653.
the host knew it to be the head of Donnbo, fa 46.
I took notice of it before u,
b. 500.
he found by me that I was no fool, b. 217.
she knew by her, L. 15

thugus aithne air.

a. in tan nach tibred duine achni ar chéli.

o. tuigfid tú ormsa ar gach aon nós gurb mé d'óglach uṁal.

go d-tuga mé ar amus mo cholla doridisi.

amus buille do thabairt air ; amus do thabairt ar níd ; do thabairt amuis ar an náṁaid.

ba egail la M. ammus long-phoirt do thabairt do Aod fair.

cia tug an t-ár mór sin orra ; is é do rigne an t-ár mór sin do thabairt orruinne.

tug bertuġad air féin a meodón a eudaiġe.

as do beul féin dobeirim breith ort.

is lór linn an breugnuġad do thugamar ar an ní sin cheana.

buillid do ṡúil do thabairt ar neach.

dobeurad caidreaṁ duit air.

aon chobair do thabairt orraib.

is maith liom an cháil dobeir tú orra ; thug sé teasdus maith ortsa.

tabair dúinn an ceartcheudfá sin ar do uile thrócaire.

tug an ceangal ceudna orrtha.

ní cóir cion stairide do thabairt air.

I took notice of it,   *b.* 500.

when a man could not recognise another.

you shall find by me upon all occasions that I am your humble servant,   *b.* 217.

that you bring me to my body again,   *fa.* 46.

attempt to strike him ; to

to attempt a thing ; to skirmish with the enemy,
      b. 511, 510, 612.

M. was afraid his camp would be attacked by Hugh,
      fa. 146.

who made that great slaughter of them ; he it is that hath made that great slaughter of us,   *dg.* 98.

he shook himself in his array,
      ob. 47.

out of thy mouth I judge thee,
      l. 18.

we think the confutation sufficient which we have given of that already,   *k.* lxiv.

to glance at one with the eye,
      b. 260.

I will make you acquainted with him,   *b.* 11.

to give you any relief,   *L.* 20.

I am glad of the good account you give of them ; he gave a good character of you,
      b. 111.

give us that due sense of all thy mercy.

he bound them in the same way,   *dg.* 94.

he ought not to get the name of historian,   *k.* liv.

tug sé do sgológaib ar chíos é;
dobeuraid sé a fíneamuin ar
chíos do sgológaib eile.

he let it out to husbandmen ;
he will let out his vineyard to
other husbandmen, *m.* 21.

tabair do grása dó an chuairt so
do thug tú air do gabáil
chuige.

give him thy grace to take this
thy visitation.

díolchuairt do thabairt air.

to pay him a visit, *b.* 258.

dobeurad cunntus duitse air.

I will give you an account of
it, *b.* 10.

'diary', conntus ar thaisdiol
laetheamail.

diary, an account of a daily
journey, *b.* 162.

caithfid geurchunntas do thabairt uatha ar son gach
bréithre díomaoinige.

they shall give a strict account
of every idle word, *d.* 484.

tuairisg iomlán do thabairt
ar thír.

to give a full description of a
country, *b.* 241.

ní b-fuil neach fá Dia le ar
féidir tuairisg do thabairt ar
na fáthaib an grád agus an
fuatha.

none but God can give an
account of the causes of
love and hatred, *b.* 9.

ar an g-ceud thuairisg dobeir
sé air féin.

at the first account he gives of
himself, *b.* 9.

tuairisg fírinneach do thabairt
ar phobul.

to give a true character of a
people, *b.* 111.

derg-ár do thabairt do Ch. for
longus Rodlaib.

dreadful slaughter was wrought
by C. on the fleet of Rod-
labh, *fa.* 152

tug sé dínsiom mór for ríg
Eirenn ; an tráth do rad
sé an dinsiom-si don ríg.

he offered a great insult to the
king of Ireland ; when he
offered this insult to the
king, *fa.* 176, 178.

drochainm do thabairt ar
neach ; ainm nach é a ainm
féin do thabairt air.

to give one a bad name ; to
call him out of his name,
b. 464.

tug sé droichdiól ar ar n-aith-
reachaib.

he treated our fathers evilly,
A. 7.

creud dobeir eagla ort?

what makes you afraid?

chum go d-tiubrad éigean ar
bochtaib.

that he might ravish the poor,
ps. 10.

níor maith liom go d-tiubrad
eurad orm.

I don't like that he should
give me a refusal, *dg.* 44.

ní dobeir fios ar súim cain-
dígeachta ar bioth.

a thing which makes known
the amount of any quantity,
b. 453.

ciad áluinn an freagra síoda
tug A. fair.

though fair was the answer A.
gave him, *fa.* 148.

ní thug sé freagra diongmála
ar bioth ar mo leabar, ní
dearna sé acht piocaireacht
air.

he gave no solid answer to my
book; he did but nibble at
it, *b.* 493.

do thugus freagra aipchíd air.

I gave him a ripe retort, *b.* 579.

níor thug sé freagra ar aon
focal dó.

he answered him to never a
word, *m.* 27.

an freagra cheudna dobeirim
ar gach sgél.

the same answer I give to
every tale, *k.* lxiv.

ní raib a fios aca cionnas
dobeuradaís freagra air;
fiachróchaid misi éinní
amáin díbsi agus tabraid
freagra orm.

neither wist they how to
answer him; I will also ask
of you one question, and
answer me, *mk.* 14, 10.

ag tabairt freagartha ar Iosa
a dubradar.

answering Jesus they said,
m. 21.

ní thug seision freagra ar bith
uirre, agus do iarradar air
ag rád ' cuir uainn í.'

he answered her not a word,
and they besought him saying send her away, *m.* 15.

níor b-féidir le haon n-duine
freagra ar bith do thabairt
air ; níor b-éidir leo freagra
do thabairt air annsna
neithib-si.

no man was able to answer
him a word ; they could not
answer him to these things,
m. 22, *l.* 14.

d'athchuinge ort, tabair gluais
muintearda air.

pray give it a benign interpre-
tation, *b.* 64.

níor b-feidir leo greim do
breith ar a foclaib; greim
do breith ar ní ;
dobeura a n-dlígead greim
orruib.

they could not take hold of his
words; to lay hold of a
thing; the law will take
hold of you, *b.* 317.

neach dobeir iasacht airgitt ar
geall.

one who gives a loan of money
for a pledge, *b.* 531

tabairtrí haráin dam ar iasacht.

lend me three loaves, *l.* 11.

d'eagla go d-tiubrad iomaith-
bior ort.

lest he reprove thee, *pr.* 30.

o. doḃeir tú masla dúinne fós.

thou reproachest us also,
l. 11.

o. innioc do thaḃairt a neach oile.

to jostle a person. *b.* 380.

ionnsaiġ maidne tugaḋ ar Eogán.

a morning attack was made on Eogan, *ob.* 308.

atá ionnsaiġe le taḃairt ar an ríġ.

an attempt is designed against the king, *b.* 44.

leasanmnaḋ do thaḃairt air.

to call him a nickname, *b.* 484.

ní féidir leat milleun do tha ḃairt orm trém' ollaṁacht chuige.

you cannot blame me for my forwardness in it, *b.* 232.

tugsat Ulaid maidm for Cinel n-Eogain ; tugsat maidm ar muintir Maoilseachlainn.

the Ulidians defeated the Kinel Owen ; they defeated the people of Maelsechlann.
fa. 128, 136.

ní ar úsáide na neithe doḃei rimse milleun ; doḃeir sé a ṁilleun soin ormsa.

it is not the use of things I blame ; he blames me foi that, *b.* 72.

gid b'é beir neiṁchion orruiḃsi is ormsa doḃeir sé neiṁ chion.

he that despiseth you despiseth me, *l.* 10.

d'éiriġ monḃur na n-Greugach do ḃríġ go d-tugthaoi neiṁ chion ar a m-baintreaḃachaiḃ 'san ministrálacht laethea ṁuil.

there arose a murmuring of the Grecians because their widows were neglected in the daily ministration,
A. 6.

tucsat trí sáiti ar Dunlang.

they made three thrusts at D.
W ars of the G. & G., 182.

an tan doḃeir sé saoirḃreith ort.

when he gives you absolution,
d. 292.

o. an tan doḃeir sé maitheaṁ nas duit.

when he forgives you, *d.* 292.

mar fuair an chnuṁ radarc air, tug sí síth sanntach sárláidir ar an athach.

when the worm caught sight of him, she gave an eager, powerful spring at the giant,
dg. 130, 138.

sáthad do thaḃairt air.

to make a thrust at him,
b. 225.

tuccaḋ seachrán an chuain orra.

they were set astray from the beach, *L.* 39.

óir is iomḋa uair doḃeiread sé siothaḋ air.

for often it had caught him, *l.* 8.

dochum slíġe do ṫaḃairt ar ṁórluaiġeacht do ṫuilleaḋ.

to give a way of meriting much, *d.* 378.

as é Brian ṫug slointe fa seach ar ḟearaiḃ Eirenn.

It is Brian that gave distinct surnames to the men of Ireland, *ob.* 430.

tarcossal mór do ṫaḃairt dóiḃ for Laigniḃ.

they offered great insult to the Leinstermen, *fa.* 136.

tugadar tarcuisne air agus do rinneadar fonoṁad faoi.

they set him at nought and mocked him, *l.* 23.

tugadar siad tarcuisne ar choṁairle Dé.

they rejected the counsel of God, *l.* 7.

doḃeuraid sé tarcuisne ar an dara fear ; taḃaraiḋ d' á ḃur n-aire nach d-taḃarṫaoi tarcuisne ar éinneach don ṁuintir ḃig-si.

he will despise the other man ; take heed that ye despise not one of these little ones, *m.* 6. 18 ; *l.* 16.

míṁeas do ṫaḃairt air.

to disparage him, *b.* 167.

míoṁod do ṫaḃairt air.

to show him disrespect.

do ṫugais maise ṁaiṫ ar ṁíoṁaise.

you have turned excellent beauty into ugliness, *dg.* 184.

solus do ṫaḃairt dó ar ní.

to give him an insight into a thing, *b.* 363.

le spioradaiḃ doḃeirid teasḃá- naḋ orra féin ann.

by spirits which show them- selves in it, *b.* 332.

ar d-taḃairt seomradóir an ríġ ar a d-toil, d'iarradar síoṫ- cháin.

having made the king's cham- berlain their friend, they desired peace, *A.* 12.

ní ṫugadar na daoine toraḋ air.

the people had no regard for him, *ob.* 483.

tuairim do ṫaḃairt ar fosglaḋ cúise éigin chum síoṫchána.

to insinuate some overtures of peace, *b.* 363.

tuairim do ṫaḃairt ar ní.

to glance upon a thing, *b.* 260.

óir doḃeirid urchóid orm.

for they do me mischief, *ps.* 55.

Dorat, he gave. *Old Irish,* with **for,** on.

dorata aithissi foir ; dorat S. aithissi foir ; at móra na haithisi doratad fort.

insults were offered to him ; S. offered him insults; great are the affronts that have been offered to thee,
Ml. 54.

ind bendacht doratad for A.

the blessing which was given to A. *Wb.* 19.

doradad fair géim druith do deunaṁ.

he was ordered to give a clown's shout, *fa.* 42.

dorat dígail foraib; duratad dígal forru.

he punished them ; vengeance was inflicted on them.
Wb. 4, 33.

dorat Crist forbairt air.

Christ gave him an increase or prosperity.

in tain dorratad grád fort.

when ordination was conferred on you, *Wb.* 28.

o. dind fortacht durat Dia dó.

of the help God gave him,
Ml. 40.

o. doratad spirut dún.

a spirit was given to us,
Wb. 21.

doratad foir a n-ainm sin.

that name was given to him,
Sg. 31.

doradad mise for altrom duit.

I was given to you in foster-age.

dorat freccra for S.
doratsat Ulaid impidi fair.
in molad doratsat na slóig fair.
dorat snáithiu coimgniu forsan scél.
an tú dorat for mo bráthair-si a dée féin do facbáil.

he answered S.
the Ulidians besought him.
the praise the hosts gave him.
he gave connecting threads to the story.
is it you that caused my brother to abandon his own gods ?

dorat Dia amus for Judaidib.

'God gave an impulse to the Jews,' *Atkinson's Hom.* 105.

doradsam faill ar ar n-aithrige.

we have neglected our penance, *fa.* 14.

doratsat in argut for tír cerdai.

they gave the money for the potter's field.

lugadar iad ar mag an phota-
dóir.

they gave them for the potter's
field.   *m.* 27.

Forms of **Dorat** after *ní, nícon, mani, nad, co, con, dia.*

ní thart, i.e. ní thug.

he did not give,   *O'Clery*

con-darta cách teist foir as
n-uisse grád foir.

that every one may bear him
testimony that he is fit to
be ordained.   *Wb.* 28.

co tardat dígal fair ; ní tharda
amus for do Choimdid ; na
tartar aimse forind itir.

that they may punish him ;
thou mayest not tempt thy
Lord ; that we be not
tempted at all.

ni co tarut Isu nach freccra
forsin errig.

Jesus gave no answer to the
ruler.

ní con tarat aithis for a chom-
nessam.

he did not offer insult to his
neighbour,   *Ml.* 36

ní tardsat nach freagra fuirri.

they did not give her any
answer.

in forend for a tardus-sa daille.

the people on whom I have
brought blindness.

dia tardsat forru fágbail in tíre.

when they made them leave
the land.

o. con dartar ainm n-apstil
dóib.

that the name of apostle is
given to them,   *Wb.* 20.

o. co tardmís-ne grád don
choimnesam.

that we should love the neighbour.

Dáilim, *and words of kindred meaning.*

rafordaled biad ocus deoch
forro   combátar   buaidir-
mesca.

meat and drink were distributed to them till they were
roaring drunk,   *LL.* 54 *b.*

ro dailed biad agus deoch
foraib.

meat and drink were distributed among them.   *od.*

o. ro dáilead flead agus feusta
dóib.

a banquet and feast were pre-
pared for them,   *dg.* 210

o. dáii do bochtaib iad.

distribute them to the poor,
s. 225.

ro dáilcad meada séime agus
leannta ro milse dóib.

mild meads and very sweet
ales were distributed to
them,   *dg.* 202.

o. ro baoi 'ga b-fodail d'á muintir.

he was dividing them among. his people. *fa.* 202.

o. noch do bronn sé dóibsean.

which he hath bestowed upon them, *Isaias,* 63.

do bríg go m-bronnann Tú do gnáth mórán tiodlaicead orm.

because Thou continually bestowest many favours on me.

má beirim an uiread sin duit, is éigean duit bonnaig maith do bronnad ormsa.

if I give you that much, you must give me a luckpenny.

culaith eudaig do bronnad air.

to give him a suit of clothes.

beatha do bronnad air.

to confer a living on him, *b.* 131.

bronnaim-se air ais ortsa leithghini mar bonn dúthracht.

I give you back half a guinea as luck-penny.

do bronnad a óige suas ar gnáthaigíde arm.

to devote his youth to the exercise of arms, *b.* 161

do bronnad suas ar Dhia.

to offer or devote to God, *b.* 161

o. do bronn sé an corp do Ióseph.

he gave the body to Joseph, *mk.* 16.

do frith an Tighearna go tiodlaiceach ort.

the Lord has been found faithful to you.

ro atchuir a fearainn air.

he gave up his lands to him, *ob.* 33.

mórán saothair do chathaṁ ar obair.

to bestow much pains on a work, *b.* 66.

go roinnead an chuid oile ar an g-cóṁdáil.

that he used to distribute the rest amongst the assembly, *k.* xxx.

do roinn sé an dá iasg orra uile.

the two fishes he divided. among them all, *mk.* 6

do roinn sé ar na deiscioblaib, agus na deisciobuil ar an muintir do bi na suíde síos iad.

he distributed them to the disciples, and the disciples to those that were seated, *j.* 6.

reac a b-fuil agad agus roinn ar na bochtaib.

sell all that thou hast and distribute to the poor, *l.* 18.

o. roinnfead-sa féin eadraib iad.

I will myself portion them out among you, *dg.* 204.

o. atá ró-fonn orm sibse d'faicsin ar ġleus go roinnfinn rib tiodlacad éigin spiorodálṫa.

I long to see you that I may impart unto you some spiritual gift, *Rom.* 1.

gabais C. ag roinn na n-uball for maithib Muṁan.

C. proceeded to divide the apples amongst the chiefs of Munster, *od.*

an té ag a b-fuil dá chóta roinnead ris an té ag nach b-fuil.

he that has two coats, let him part to him who has none, *l.* 3.

o. do roinn sé don beag do bía aco friu.

he distributed part of their small provisions amongst them, *ob.* 207.

o. ár maoin do roinn ris na bochtaib.

to share our goods with the poor, *d.* 162.

a. méit donindnagar fornni fochith.

what ever tribulation is sent to us.

o. an tan do bris mé na cúig aráin ar na cúig ṁíle.

when I broke the five loaves among the five thousand, *mk.* 8.

o. canfad chum an Tiġearna do bríġ gur roinn sé go fialṁar riomsa.

I will sing unto the Lord because he had dealt generously with me, *ps.* 13.

o. is mar so do rinne an Tiġearna rium.

thus hath the Lord dealt with me, *l.* 1.

o. do roinn sé ré crannchar a b-fearann dóib.

he divided their land to them by lot, *A.* 13.

o. abair rem' dearbráthair an oiġreacht do roinn rium; do roinn seision a ṁaoin eatorra (roinn é orra a chuid—*Scotch Testam.*)

tell my brother to divide the inheritance with me; he divided his living unto them, *l.* 12, 15.

do roinneadar iad ar gach aon fá leith do réir a riachdanuis.

they parted them to all men as every man had need, *A.* 2, 4.

roinn ar dó.

to divide in two, *od.*

nach roinnid Sliġe Asail Míde for dó?

does not Slighe Asail divide Meath into two parts? *fa.* 176

roinnid sé an chruinne ar a dó go díreach.

it divides the globe into two equal parts, *b.* 415.

o. ag roinn do gach aon fó leith do réir mar as áil ris.

dividing severally to every man as he will, 1 *Cor.* 12.

o. cuirid se fonn orruinn ar maoin do roinn go fálṁair ris na bochtaib.

it inclines us to share our goods freely with the poor *d.* 161.

iompoiġ, o m'anam, chum do ṡuaiṁneasa, óir do fríth an Tiġearna go tiodlaictheach ort.

O my soul, turn again unto thy rest, for the Lord hath been found bountiful to thee, *ṗ.* 116.

o. biaid tusa tiodlaiceach daṁ.

thou wilt be bountiful to me, *ṗ.* 142.

Cuirim, I put.

cuirim ort a hucht Dé bí, innsin dúinn.

I adjure thee by the living God that thou tell us, *m.* 26.

cuirim a hucht Dé ort gan mo phianad.

I adjure thee by God not to torment me, *mṫ.* 5.

o. cuirmíd fá ġeasaib sib.

we adjure you, *A.* 19.

cuirim ar do choġuas.

I call your conscience to witness, *b.* 99.

bochtacht do chuireas ornn é do deunad.

poverty drives us to do it, *b.* 489.

do chur air.

to persuade him, *b.* 534.

o. dob urus é do chur chuige.

it was easy to persuade him to do it, *b.* 534.

ná cuiread an ní sin ort.

let not that thing displease you. *cṫ.* 148.

cuirid sin orm go gar.

that closely concerns me, *b.* 488.

do chuir sin go mór ar Lir ; nocha g-cuirfid orraib a beith in bar n-eunaib.

that preyed greatly on Lir; ye shall not be distressed at being birds, *Lir §§. 5. 10. 20.*

an beag agaibsi daoine do chur ?

is it a small thing for you to weary men ? *Isaias 7.*

is mór chuireas an ní sin orm.

that sticks to my heart. *b.* 303.

tá sé ag cur orm

he is afflicting me. *cṫ.*

tá an ṁuir ag cur orm

the sea is making me sick

is beag do chuiread sé orm siúbal ar chois go Luimneach.

I would think little of going on foot to Limerick.

ní féidir le reusún a chur
ormsa éinní don t-sórt sin
do chieidiomuin.

do chur air d'á aimdeoin ní do
deunam ; ag cur ar chách.

d'á chur foraib

aitheonaid sé nach b-fuil
éifeacht ann a'r cuiread ort.

creud an maith chuireas an
aithne-si orrainn do deunam?

do chuir gnáthad na guasachta a mothúgad a n-dearmad
air.

do chuir sé so leis do bárr ar
gach ní.

cuirid sí do choingioll orra.

ní chuirfead-sa an sáimrige sin
do díoth ort.

, do chuir an t-anfad d'éigean
air do seolad asteach chum
cuain is feárr d'feudfad sé.

d'iarradar air gan a chur d'-
fiachaib orra dul an sa
dubaigeun.

do chuireadar d'fiachaib ar
óglach áirigthe do bí ag gabáil tharrsa a chroch
d'iomchar,

cuirid d'fiachaib orraib an tim-
cheallgearrad do gabáil
chuige.

do chuir sé d'fiachaib ar a
deisciopluib dul a luing.

cuir d'fiachaib ar na daoinib
suíde síos.

do chuireadar d'fiachaib air a
deunam ; cuirfid mise d'fiá-
chaib ort é ; chuirfead d'fiachaib orrainn a deunad.

reason can't force me to believe anything of that kind,
b. 357.

to force him to do a thing ;
huffing people, *b.* 229, 328.

to accuse them of it,
4 *Masters*, year 1574.

he shall know that there is
nothing in what has been
imputed to you, *A.* 21.

what good doth this commandment oblige us to do ? *d.* 92.

the usualness of the danger
has made him lose the
sense of it, *b.* 653.

he added this yet above all, *l.*3.

she obliges them.

I will not rob you of that
pleasure, *b.* 584.

the storm forced him to make
for harbour as best he could
b. 559, 441.

they besought him that they
would not command them
to go into the deep *l.* 8

they compelled a certain youth
who passed by to bear his
cross, *mk.* 15.

they constrain you to receive
circumcision, *Gal.* 6.

he constrained his disciples to
get into a boat, *m.* 14

make the men sit down.

they forced him to to do it ;
I will make you do it ; it
may engage us to do it.

cuirfid me d'ualach ortsa a deunam; cuirim d'ualach ort é; ó tá go g-cuireann sé d'ualach air.

I will oblige you to do it; I insist on your doing it; since it requires of him.

do chonncas dúinn gan ní as mó d'ualach do chur orruib ná na neithe riachtana so.

it seemed good to lay upon you no greater burden than these necessary things, *A.* 15.

cuirfead fá deara air a focal do sheunad.

I will make him deny his word, *b.* 182.

cuir fá deara ar phobul do réigeachad; cuir fá deara air aire ar a chúrum.

make the people to agree; compel him to mind his business, *b.* 128.

cuirfead fa deara air fonn oile do chantain.

I will make him sing another tune, *b.* 399.

o. cuirid an bochtaine fá deara dó iarratus do deunam.

poverty compels him to beg, *b.* 128.

fáth chuireas fá deara ar neach ní éigin do deunad.

a cause which makes a person do a certain thing, *b.* 350.

ealadna agus fogluim do chur ar agaid; easárd do chur ar agaid.

to promote arts and sciences; to foment a sedition, *b.* 554, 226.

ag iarraid do glóire-se do chur ar agaid.

seeking to advance thy glory.

ar mod go g-cuirfide do glóir-se ar agaid.

so that thy glory shall be advanced.

so do níd fa deara do Dháibid eolus Dé do chur ar agaid.

this caused David to promote the knowledge of God.

céard do chur ar agaid.

to force a trade, *b.* 229.

cuir ar ár n-agaid sinn le do chuidiúgad gnáthach.

prosper us with thy constant assistance.

obair do chur ar a hagaid.

to help a business forward, *b.* 308.

cuirfid so d'obair ar agaid go rómór.

this will forward your work very much, *b.* 232.

ní do chur ar agaid; an cogad do chur ar agaid.

to accelerate a thing, to set a a thing on foot; to carry on the war, *b.* 105, 8, 227.

an t-síothcháin do chur ar agaid.

to mediate the peace, *b.* 454

is mór an fear chum fogluma do chur ar agaid é.

he is a great encourager of learning, *b.* 352.

do chur ar aiṁleas.

a g-cur ar a n-aire níos feárr;
neach do chur ar airechas
roiṁ rae.

taréis a cor ar a hais.

cuir thú féin ar aithearrach
chrotha.

slíġe an Tiġearna do chur ar
anáird.

ro cuiread an t-aonach ar athlá.

an t-saoirbreith do chur ar
cháirde nó ar athlá dó.

do chuir sé ar athlá iad.

an ṁórthrócaire-se do chur ar
biseach chum chuir ar
aġaid do ṡoisgéil.

cuir ar n-a boġad é.

is é chuireas an ingréim ar
bun; coláiste do chur ar bun.

an tan do chuir sé an t-sácra-
muint-se ar bun.

an te chuireas an t-aodaire ar
cáirde; bíoc go g-cuirfead ar
n-iarratus ar cáirde.

cuirid measardacht duine a
ḟearg ar cáirde.

chum gan a g-cur níos faide ar
cáirde d'a thaob so.

an duine do chuirfead a leas ar
cáirde ó ló go lá.

do chur ar ceall.

a. ġilla do chur ar cend Aeda.

aduḃradar gurab í ro chuir
ar cheann chuirp Dh.

do chuireas ar chionn leabar
iomlán é, agus do chuir sé
sé leabair neiṁiomlána
chugam.

---

to pervert, 　　b. 534.

making them more vigilant;
to put one on his guard beforehand, 　　b. 107

after she had been sent back,
ob. 129.

disguise yourself, 　ob. 141.

to pervert the way of the Lord.

the gathering was put off, dg. 44.

to defer giving him absolution
d. 292, 294.

he deferred them, 　A. 24.

to improve this great mercy to
the advancement of thy
gospel.

steep it, 　　b. 623.

it is he that originates the
persecution; to found a
college, 　b. 233, 352.

when he instituted this sacra-
ment, 　　d. 246.

he whom the pastor puts off
for a time; though he should
defer granting our request,
d. 142, 376.

the moderation of a man de-
ferreth his anger, 　pr. 19.

not to send them farther off
touching this point, 　d. xi.

the man who would defer his wel-
fare from day to day, d. 354.

to cloud, 　　b. 120.

to send a servant to Aed.

they said it was she that sent
for the body of D. dg. 200.

I sent him for perfect books,
and he sent me imperfect
ones, 　　b. 345.

clog do chur ar chrochad.

ar do laiṁ cuirim coiṁeud m'anma.

do chuireadar ar choiṁeud an Tiġearna, ionn a'r chreideadar, iad.

do ṡeoladar go Antióchia, an áit as ar' cuiread ar chóiṁeud ġrás Dé iad chum na hoibre do chóiṁlíonadar.

a g-cur ar a g-coiṁeud níos feárr ó sin suas.

do chuir sé teachta ar cenn Cionaoith.

teachtaireaḋa tairisi do chur ar cenn na ritaire.

agus do imthiġ sé roiṁe ar n-a chur ar comairce ġrás Dé do na bráithrib ; cuirim sib ar cumairce Dé.

soiġdiuiride do chur ar coiṁnid.

is maith churthaoi ar g-cúl aithne Dé, ionnas go g-coiṁeudfad sib bur n-gnáthuġad féin ; ag cur bréithre Dé ar g-cúl.

gideaḋ, ó churththaoi ar g-cúl í agus go m-beirthí do breith nach fiú sib an beatha ṁarthannach d'faġáil.

fóirneart do chur a g-cúl le fóirneart oile ; éiriceacht do chur ar g-cúl ; do chur ar g-cúl; dliġead do chur ar g-cúl.

chum gach uile scrupuil do chur ar g-cúl

cuirid an ġaoth thuaith an fearthainn ar g-cul.

to hang a bell, *b.* 292.

into thy hands I commend my soul, *d.* 414.

they commended them to the Lord, in whom they believed, *A.* 14.

they sailed to Antioch, from whence they had been recommended to the grace of God for the work which they fulfilled, *A.* 14.

making them more cautious for the future.

he sent messengers for Cionaoth, *fa.* 116.

to send trusty messengers to the knights *fa.* 170.

he departed, being recommended by the brethren to to the grace of God ; I commend you to God, *A.* 15. 20.

to billet soldiers, *b.* 70.

full well ye reject the commandment of God, that ye may keep your own tradition ; making the word of God of none effect, *mk.* 7.

but, seeing that ye put it from you and judge yourselves unworthy of everlasting life, *A.* 13.

to repel force by force ; to extirpate heresy ; to discountenance ; to abolish a law, *b.* 228, 202, 165, 4.

to take away all scruple.

the north wind drives away rain, *pr.* 25.

do bríġ gur chuir tú an t-eolus
ar g-cúl cuirſe mise thúsa ar
g-cúl mar an g-ceudna.

because thou hast neglected
knowledge I will also reject
thee, *d.* 334.

cid bé ní do cuiread ar g-cúl
ann.

whatever hath been been de-
cayed in him.

creud fá'r cuiread cuid díob ar
g-cúl agus a b-ſuil cuid ar
congbáil ?

why have some of them been
abolished and some re-
tained ?

cuirim ar g cúl.

I cancel, I annul, *ob.* 148.

ní chuirſe so go bráth mo ġrád
ar g-cúl ris,

this will never make me out of
love with him, *b.* 441.

go d-tiocfad chum críche go
g-cuirſíde ar g-cúl a mór-
dacht-sa.

that it would come to pass that
her magnitude should
be destroyed, *a.* 19.

ionnas go g-cuirfead sé an
ġeallaṁain ar g-cúl.

so that it should make the
promise to be of no effect,
Gal. 3.

leannta na seilge do chur ar
g-cúl.

to lay the vapours of the
spleen, *b.* 398.

ní do chur ar chuṁdach duine
oile.

to deposit a thing with another
person, *b.* 158.

do chuir sé deachtuġad iomlán
an chogaid ar a chúrum ;
ní do chur ar a chúrum.

he committed the whole man-
agement of the war to his
charge ; to commit a thing
to his charge. *b.* 111

ní do chur ar churum duine
eile.

to deliver a thing to another's
trust, *b.* 67.

cuirid an sionnach na gadair
ar deirid.

the fox casts off the dogs,
b. 106.

curtha ar deoruiġeacht.

sent into exile, *b.* 200.

do chur ar díbirt.

to relegate, banish, *b.*

do chur ar díoth.

to frustrate, *b.* 238

do chur ar díoth daoine.

to depopulate, *b.* 158.

duine do chur ar éisteacht.

to arraign a person, *b.* 37.

long do chur ar eolus.

to pilot a ship, *b.* 421.

soiġdiuiride curthar ar ſéidm
ġuasachtaiġ.

soldiers who are put to dangerous service, *b.* 230.

do chur amach ar iasacht.

to put out to loan, *b.* 420.

do chur ar n-ionntód.

to upset, tumble, *b.* 645.

nach féidir a chur ar láiṁ
duine oile.

which cannot be alienated,
b. 349.

do chur ar leataoib.
to lay aside, *b.* 398.

do chur ar lár.
to demolish, *b.* 157.

is lór é chum an domain do chur ar dearglasaḋ ; an t-iomlán do chur ar lasaḋ.
it is enough to set the world in a flame ; to set all in a flame, *b.* 220.

do chur ar lear.
to alienate, *b.* 349.

go g-cuiriḋ Dia ar do leas thu!
God speed you well ! *b.* 618.

neach do chur ar a leas.
to move one to good, *b.* 475

do chuirfeaḋ sé neach ar leirg a ḋrochṁian.
it would make a person addicted to lust, *b.* 432.

sluaġ do chur ar leathnúġaḋ geiṁre.
to put an army in winter quarters, *b.* 37.

do chur ar leith.
to lay aside, *b.* 39.

cuiriḋ ar leith ḋaṁ Saul fá chóṁair na hoibre chum ar' ġoir mé é.
separate me Saul for the work whereunto I have called him, *A.* 13.

cia chuireas ar leith thu ?
who discerneth thee, 1 *Cor.* 4.

cuir ar lúġ í.
cock it (the gun), *Scotch.*

ag cur ar maill.
deferring, *b.* 155.

ná cuir-se mé ar mearball.
do not set me astray, *dg.* 156.

do chur ar mearuġaḋ.
to disorder. *b.* 166.

cuiriḋ an fearg an aigne ar mearuġaḋ.
anger ruffles the mind, *b.* 588.

do chur ar meisge.
to inebriate, *b.* 356, 176.

do chur ar misgiḋ.
to make drunk, *b.* 238.

do chur ar míoáird ; do chur ar miochóir.
to put out of order ; to hurry, *b.* 516, 331.

neach do chur ar mire.
to make one mad

cuiriḋ se ar mire mé faicsin na heugcóra do níthear air.
he sets me mad to see how he is wronged, *b.* 437, 439.

neach do chur ar mire lé dúil an ní.
to set a person agog, *b.* 267.

do chur a muda.
to destroy.

do chur ar muin a chéile.
to put in a heap, *b.* 302.

do chur ar neaṁchuiṁne.
to bury in oblivion, *b.* 92.

ní do chur ar neiṁní.
to defeat a thing, *b.* 154.

an uile ḋliġeaḋ do chur ar neiṁní.
to nullify, reverse, abolish all law, *b.* 89, 603.

do chur ar neiṁni ; *o.* do chur a neiṁni.
to set at nought, *b.* 501.

do chuireadar do dliġead ar neiṁni.

do chur ar órduġaḋ.

do chur ar ne.ṁórduġaḋ.

soiġdiúiríde do chur ar rolla.

do chur ar saobnós, mur d'ól-fad neach deoch go hiomurcach san maidin.

do chuir sé uaḋ a éinġein Mhic ar an t-saoġal chum go mairfead sinne thríd.

cia chruthaiġ agus do chuir ar an t-saoġal thu?

do chuir Dia a Mhac ar an t-saoġal.

oiġreacht do chur ar scaipiḋ.

gach toirmeasg do chuirfead ar seachrán sinn.

neach do chuir ar seachrán as an slíġe.

a theangaid do chur ar siúbal.

neach do chur ar siúbal;

do chuir mé ar siúbal é.

do thionnsgain an fear-sa obair do chur ar siúbal agus níor féd sé críoch do chur uirre.

do chuir sé an chóiṁthionól ar siúbal.

dauirseach do chur ar sgaoil.

long du chur amach ar snáṁ.

cuirim mo leaba ar snáṁ.

do chuir an tráġ ar sonchrith.

amail nachada duine d'a chur ar threisi agus ar thricce.

---

they have destroyed thy law,
ps. 119.

to depute, *b.* 158.

to put out of order, *b.* 516.

to enroll soldiers, *b.* 417.

to maudle, as one would drink to excess in the morning,
b. 450.

he sent his only begotten Son into the world that we might live through Him,
1 *John*, 4.

who created and placed you in the world? *d.* 8.

God sent his Son into the world,

to make havoc of an inheritance, *b.* 299.

every obstacle that might lead us astray.

to lead one out of the way,
b. 399.

to set his tongue going, *b.* 117.

to dismiss; to send a person a grazing, *b.* 166, 275.

I put him to the run, *b.* 589.

this man began to build, and was not able to finish,
l. 14.

he dismissed the assembly,
A. 19.

to give liberty to a slave,
b. 445.

to set a ship afloat, *b.* 17.

I set my bed afloat, *ps.* 6.

he caused the shore to reverberate, *dg.* 94.

as if another man were putting him to his strength and dexterity, *ja.* 24.

neach d'á chuir féin ar teithe.	to take to one's heels, *b.* 306.
do chuaiḋ sé amach lé héirġe an laoi do chur lucht oibre ar tuarasdal ann aḟíneaṁuin.	he went out early in the morning to hire labourers into his vineyard, *m.* 20.
do chur ar uiṁir na ḃ-fomósach náttúrtha ; do chur asteach ar uiṁir na naoṁ.	to put in the number of natural subjects, to naturalize ; to canonize, *b.* 486, 101.
neach d'á chur féin ar uiṁir soiġdiúriḋe.	to enlist as a soldier, *b.* 362.
go g-cuiriḋ Dia an t-áḋ agus an ráḋ ort!	God prosper you !
is chum aḋnáire do chur orraiḃ adeirim so.	I speak this to your shame, 1 *Cor.* 15.
aġaiḋ ṁaith do chur ar ḋrochluithche.	to put a good face on a bad game, *b.* 268
ainḟiacha nó anluach do chur air.	to overrate or overprice it, *b.* 520.
do chuir sé airchis orra.	he sent to meet them, *ob.* 14.
ní chuireann sé áird ar a ḟios do ḃeith aige.	he regards not to know it, *pr.* 29.
níor chuir sé mórán aire uirri, ná cuir aire orra ; do chuir sé a chuid airgitt ar neithiḃ dioṁaoine.	he did not much need her ; don't mind them ; he bestowed his money on idle things, *b.* 66.
ag cur áir orraiḃ.	slaughtering them, *dg.* 104.
do sgeithius amach focal noch chuireas aithṁeula mo chroíḋe orm.	I blurted out a word, of which I heartily repent, *b.* 77.
aṁgar do chur air.	to molest him, *b.* 469.
do chur anchumaḋ ar a ḃeul.	to mow. *b.* 477.
aithne do chur air.	to put a brand upon him, *b.* 84.
do chuirfinn m'anam air.	I would lay my life on it, *b.* 410.
tabair dúinne atá ag cur athchuinge ort.	grant to us who implore thee.
cuirmíd d'impíde agus d'athchuinge orraib toil Dé do ḋeunaṁ.	we beseech and exhort you to do God's will, 1 *Thess.* 4.
gach anró do chuireaḋ sé orrainn.	every misery he may inflict on us.

a. ro cuiread ár ar Gallaib.
do chuir se bac orra.
do chur bail ar a sparán.
ro chuiris an báire air.

ballad do chur ar baile.

bannuíde síothchána do chur air.
cia agaibsi feudas aon bann-láṁ aṁáin do chur ar áirde féin?
an m-bía beann aige ar do ṡaiḋbrios? ná cuiread beann air.
cuir do beannuġud orra-sa.
is do chur adnáire orraib do labraim;
do thóg Dia neithe éigcríonna an t-sáoġail chum adnáire do chur ar na daoinib eagnuiḋe.
gan beann do chur air.
do chur an breitheaṁnais sgríobtha a g-críċ orro.

má bíonn an salann gan blas creud lé g-cuirfide blas air?

bólta do chur ar an dorus; breitheaṁnas aithriġe do chur air.
an té chuireas breug air.
bruiġean do chur air.
na bain leis, na cuir buairead air.
buair do chur air.
na cuir buaidread ort féin, óir ní fiú misi go rachfá asteach fá chleith mo thiġe.

the English were defeated.
he hindered them,   *ob.* 34.
to husband his purse,   *b.* 332.
you won the game against him,   *dg.* 56.
to put a wall round a place,
    b. 243.
to bind him to the peace.

which of you can add to his stature one cubit?   *l.* 12.

will he esteem thy riches? let him not regard it,
    Job 36. 3.
give thy blessing to these.
I say this to move you to shame;
God hath chosen the foolish things of the world to confound the wise, *I. Cor.* 6, 1.

not to take notice of it, *b.* 500.
to carry out the written judgment against them,
    ps. 142.
if the salt be without savour, wherewith shall it be seasoned?   *l.* 14.
to bolt the door; to impose a penance on him,   *d.* 284.

he who slanders him, *b.* 172,62.
to pick a quarrel with him.
don't meddle with him, *b.* 453.

to molest him,   *b.* 469.
do not trouble thyself, for I am not worthy that thou shouldst enter under my roof,   *l.* 7.

creud an buairead chuireas
soin ortsa? cuirid an sgeui-
sa buairead mór orm.

o. do ġníḋ bolaiḋ an tabaca
buaireaḋ ḋaṁsa.

do chur buaiḋeartha ar an b-
pobul.

na cuir buaireaḋ orm, atá glas
ar an dorus.

buaireaḋ do chur air, do chur
buairiṁ air; péistéog chuireas buaireaḋ ar daoiniḃ.

creud fá g-cuirthí buaireaḋ
uirre?

fuair th' inġean bás, ná
cuir buaireaḋ ar an ṁai-
ġisdir.

cáin do chuireadar ar na
Saxaiḃ; as cáin sin chuireas
an chinneaṁuin orm.

má's teacht ḋaṁ cuirfead a
g-céill a ġníoṁartha do
ġní sé, ag cur callóide orruinn ré briathraiḃ urchói-
deacha.

cuir carbad ar ḋá each díoḃ.

atá Dia fírinneach nach ḃ-fuil-
eongaiḋ cathuġaḋ do chur
orruiḃ ós ceann ḃur neirt.

do chuireadar caoincóir ar a
g-coṁráḋ.

agus dream eile ag cur chath-
uiġthe air do iarradar
córṁartha ó neaṁ air.

creud fá a g-cuirthí cathuġaḋ
orm? do chuireadar ḃur
n-aithre cathuġaḋ orm.

what need you care? this news
put me in a great maze or
mess, *b.* 489, 451.
the smell of tobacco offends
me, *b.* 510.
to stir up the people, *A.* 17.

trouble me not, the door is
now shut, *l.* 11.
to discomfort or incommode
him, to give him trouble; an
insect that annoys men,
b. 165, 92, 259.
why trouble ye her? *mk.* 14

thy daughter is dead, do not
trouble the master, *l.* 8.

a tribute which they imposed
on the Saxons; it is a fine
that fortune puts on me,
b. 150.
if I come I will remember his
deeds which he doeth,
prating against us with
malicious words,
3rd Ep. of John.
yoke two horses of them to
a chariot, *dg.* 60.
God is faithful who will not
suffer you to be tempted
above your strength,
1 *Cor.* 10.
they gave fair words, *b.* 72.

and others tempting him
sought of him a sign from
heaven, *l.* 11.
why tempt ye me? your
fathers tempted me,
m. 22, *ps.* 95.

ceangal pósda do chur air féin — to enter into the bonds of matrimony, *b.* 449.

cuirfir mé mar cheann orra. — thou wilt make me their head.

an té ar a m-bí croíde acbreach cuirid sé ceannairg ar siúbal — he that hath a proud heart stirreth up strife, *pr.* 28.

do bí eagla orra ceist do chur airsion. — they were afraid to ask him a question, *l.* 9.

do cuiread an cheist ormsa. — the question was put to me.

o. do cuiread an cheist chugamsa. — the question was sent to me.

an tan chuirfeas ceist ort. — when he shall put a question to you, *d.* 290.

do leanadar ag cur na ceiste sin air, — they continued asking him.

aithnigmíd nach rigeann tú a leas duine ar bith do chur ceiste ort. — we recognize that thou needest not that any man should ask thee.

do chuir sé ceist orra ar an t-slíge ag rád riu; do chuireadar ceist fá'n ní ceudna sin air; níor lám éineach ó sin suas ceist do chur air. — he asked them, by the way, saying unto them; they asked him about the same matter; no man after that durst ask him any question, *mk.* 8, 10, 12.

ag éisteacht riu agus ag cur ceast orra. — hearing them and asking them questions, *l.* 2.

is í so mo freagra don druing chuirfeas ceist orm. — this is my answer to them who shall examine me, 1 *Cor.* 9.

o. ar g-ceasdúgad an lucht coimeuda dó. — having examined the keepers *A.* 12.

an cionnta do chur ar neach oile. — to lay the fault on another, *b.* 398.

cuirid sí a clann ar duine oile. — she imputes her children to another man, *b.* 210.

cuirid sé cleas orra. — he cheats them, *b.* 74.

do geabainn óm' chroíde cluain do chur air; do chur cluaine air; cluainearacht do chur ar mnaoi. — I could find it in my heart to play him a trick; to fawn upon him; to flatter a woman, *b.* 303, 211, 246.

cuiread sé a chloídeam ar a thaob. — let him pnt his sword by his side. *ex.* 3 2.

do chuir F. an cluitche ar O. san riocht g-ceudna.

an té chuireas coir bréige air.

coir gráineamhail do chur air.

no go b-fagad sé ionad ar é féin do glanad ón g-coir do chuirfide air.

agus nach n-deuntaoi coir do chur ort.

neach do chur coimirce a anma air.

do chuir se comaoin mór ormsa ; do chuir tú comaoin orm ; níor déarnaig sé aon chomaoin do chur orm ; comaoine do chur air,

atámaoid ag cur cómarthaid air lé chómartha na croiche.

cómartha do chur air.

do chuir sé comhgairm ar a maithib.

do chur córad ar ní.

do thionnsgnadar conspóid do chur air.

cuirid an chríoch coróin ar an obair.

ci b'é ní chuireas corruide ar do súilib ; na daoine chuir corruide orraib.

do chuir tú corruíge orm ; cuirid sé corruide uirre.

bud maith leis cosamhlacht ceirt do chur ar a eugcóir.

cosg do chur ar loingeas ; cosg curthar ar loingeas gan dul amach as cuan ; cuirid tú cosg orm óm' obair.

F. tnrned the game against O in the same manner, dg. 144.

he who falsely accuses him.

to bring a heinous charge against him, b. 398.

until he should have an opportunity of clearing himself of the crime laid against him, A. 25.

and that you may not be accused.

to put one's life into his hands b. 410.

he has greatly obliged me; you have done me a favour; he did not oblige me at all ; to oblige him, b. 313, 211, 402, 504.

we do sign him with the sign of the cross.

to cast a brand upon him, b. 8.

he convoked their chiefs, b. 121.

to garnish a thing. b. 249.

they began to question with him, mk. 8.

the end crowns the work, b. 196.

whatsoever doth offend thine eyes; those who have offended you.

you startled me.

he vexes her, b. 309.

he thought well to give an appearance of justice to his injustice.

to lay an embargo on ships; prohicition which is put on vessels not to go out of port; you hinder me from my work, b. 341, 314.

cuirid cosg ar bur n-armaib; níor b-féidir leis cosg do chur air.

restrain your weapons; he could not hinder him,
dg. 160, 208.

cosg curthar ar níd.

an obstacle which is put to a thing, *b.* 506.

ag cur críche ar a chathuiġthib don diabal.

when the devil had ended all his temptations, *l.* 4.

go g-cuirfid sé críoch air.

that he will perform it, *Phil* 1.

cia agaibsi duine, lé mad mian tor do deunaṁ, nach suídfead ar tús do theilgean cuntuis an chosduis, an m-biad acfuinn aige chum críche do chur air; agus gan cumas aige críoch do chur air.

which of you is there, intending to build a tower, that would not sit down first to count the cost whether he have sufficient to finish it; and not being able to finish it, *l.* 14.

cuirid oṁan an báis critheagla air.

the fear of death terrifies him.

critheagla do chur air; critheagla do chur ar a spioraidiġe.

to put him in a fret; to damp his spirits, *b.* 237, 149.

cuirfid sé criothnúġad air.

it will frighten him.

ná cuirid bur g-croide air.

set not your heart upon it, *ps.* 62.

cuibreach láṁ do chur air chimiochaib a g-carcair.

to manacle captives in prison. *b.* 442.

ní hionnan cuiread do chur ar an m-bás agus a ionnsaiġe.

it is not the same thing to invite death and to meet it.

do thionnsgnadar cúis do chur air.

they began to accuse him, *l.* 24.

cad í an chúis chuirthí ar an duine so?

what accusation bring ye against this man?

c'áit a b-fuil an ṁuintir úd do chuir cúis ort?

where are thine accusers? *j.* 8.

an té lé'r ab aill cúis breitheaṁnuis do chur ort, agus do chóta do buain díot, léig leis do chlóca fós.

if any man will sue thee at the law and take away thy coat, let him have thy cloak also, *m.* 5.

conntus ar neithib ar bith do chur a sgríbinn.

to make a list of things, *b.* 417.

ná cuir curad ar spiorad Dé.

oppose no obstacle to the spirit of God, *ob.* 153.

do chuiridis na daoine tinne ar na sráidíb.

a. dochorastar Dia deilb mór-draige air.

an uair do chuir sé deiread ar labairt le S.

do cuiread deistion ar fiaclaib na cloinne.

an dream ar a g-cuirthear dí-birt fá an g-creideaṁ fíre do chosnaṁ.

do chuir sé díon air.

do chur dochair air.

do chur dóchuis ar scath aoin oile.

o. atá mo dóchus ionnatsa ; *o.* atá mo ṁuinígin as-sadsa.

o. do chuireas muinígin ṁor ann.

atá a g-cuiṁne ag cur doláis orm.

doilġíos do chur air.

do chuireadar doilġeas air annsa b-fásach.

ná cuirid doilġeas ar Spiorad Naoṁtha Dé, lé'r cuiread seula orraib go lá an fuas-laigthe.

drochbail do chur ar ní.

na l ochta chuireas drochbáil air.

droichṁisneach iomlán do chur air.

drochthásg do chur air.

do chur droichtheasdais air.

drochthuairisg do chur air.

they laid the sick in the streets, *mk.* 6.

God put into him a form oi great folly.

when he had made an end ot speaking to S.

the children's teeth were numbed.

such as are banished for main-taining the true faith, *d.* 204.

he covered it, *ob.* 134.

to grate upon him, *b.* 273.

to repose trust in another.

I rely upon you ; I rely upon you, *b.*

I reposed great trust in him.

the remembrance of them is grievous to me.

to discomfort him, to break his heart, *b.* 303, 165.

they grieved him in the desert, *ps.* 78.

grieve not the Holy Spirit of God whereby ye have been sealed unto the day of re-demption, *Ephes.* 4.

to waste, lavish, mismanage a thing, *b.* 396, 465.

the defects that render it void.

to put him quite out of heart, *b.* 303.

to fix an evil report on him, *b.* 219.

to calumniate him, *b.* 100.

to cast an aspersion on him, *b.* 40.

do chuirfeá an dub 'na ġealormsa.

you would make me believe
that black was white, *b.* 112.

do chuir sé eagla mór oruinn;
eagla mór do chur air.

he put us in great fear; to put
him in great fear,
b. 211, 495.

o. eaglaiḋeadar tuilte na neiṁdiachta mé.

the overflowings of ungodliness have made me afraid,
ps. 18.

cuir eagla orra.

put them in fear, *ps.* 9.

do chuir sé eagla ar gach
beitheach do tharla leis.

he put fear into every animal
he met.

o. cuirid sin oṁan um' chroíḋe.

it makes my heart ache, *b.* 303.

ná cuir éigean ort féin.

don't strain yourself. *b.* 625.

dochum eoluis do chur air.

in order to know him, *d.* 8.

eud do chur air.

to make him jealous, *b.* 336.

cuiriḋ eagla an Tiġearna fad
ar na laethiḃ.

the fear of the Lord prolongeth days, *pr.* 10.

do chuir se failc air.

he broke his jaw, *ob.* 228.

chuir í fáilt air Ealasaid.

she saluted Elizabeth,
l. 1. *Scotch.*

cuir faire ar mo beul.

set a watch before my mouth,
ps. 141.

cuirfiḋ sé faobar ar a chlaoidiḃ.

he will whet his sword, *ps.* 7.

do chur feirge air; fearg do
chur air.

to embitter him; to put him in
a fret, *b.* 237, 341.

cuirthear fearg air gach aon lá.

he is provoked every day,
ps. 76.

gan fearg do chur ort.

not to offend thee.

do ḋeonuiġ tú fearthainn aoibinn do chur chugainn ar hoiġreacht féin.

thou hast been pleased to send
a joyful rain on thine inheritance.

neach do chuireas órduġaḋ
agus feisde ar ṁuinntirthíġe.

one who regulates and entertains a household, *b.* 509.

do chuir sé fiacha air féin.

he contracted debts, *b.* 152.

cuirim a fiadnuise orruibse andiu go b-fuilim glan ó fuil.

I take you to record this day
that I am pure from blood,
A. 20.

feilc, íoḋon, filleaḋ suas do
curthar ar cheinnbeirt.

cock, that is, a turn up that
is given to a hat, *b.* 122.

fíonáil do chur air.

to fine him.

do chuir a Thiġearna fios air-
sean ; do chuireadar fios ar
fead na tíre sin uile ar gach
taob díob.

ro chuir-siom fios ar a n-amus
saide.

an do buain a b-fuil aguinn
dínn do chuireabar fios
orruinn ?

do chuir Ióseph fios ar a
athair agus ar a lucht gaoil
uile.

cuir fios ar bainne agus ar im
gus an lachtairm ; ar chuiris
fios ar an d-tobac dam?
cuirfead fios air.

do chuir sé fios ar an g-cuid
oile do muintír Fhinn.

cuir fir ar Ioppa agus cuir fios
ar Shíomón d'arab cómainm
Peadar; fuair sé fógra ó Dhia
fios do chur ortsa d'a thíġ
féin ; do chuir mé fios ortsa
agus as maith do rinne tú
teacht.

do chuir sé fios ar Phól agus éist
sé ris a d-timcheall an chreidim a g-Chríost ; an uair
bias uain agamsa air cuirfid
mé fios ort ; ag cur feasa air
go minic do labrad sé ris ;
go g-cuirfead fios air go h-
Ierusalem.

chuir G. feasa agus teachta ar
cheann a chloinne.

is fá an ádbar soin do chuir
mé fios orruibse cum bur
b-icicsine agus labartha rib.

o. níl fíos agam ar éinní de.

o. cuir fios aige.

his lord sent for him; they
sent out into all that
country round about them,
                              m. 18, 14.
he sent for them,   fa. 178.

is it to take away from us all
we have ye have called us ?
                              Judges, 14.
Joseph sent and called his
father to him and all his
kindred,   A. 7.
send for butter and milk to
the dairy ; did you send for
the tobacco for me ? I will
send for it.
he sent for the rest of Finn's
people,   dg. 162.
send men to Joppa and call
for Simon whose surname is
Pe.er ; he was warned by
God to send for thee into
his house ; I sent to thee
and thou hast well done
that thou hast come,
                              A. 10, 11.
he sent for Paul and heard
him concerning the faith in
Christ ; when I have a con-
venient season I will call
for thee ; sending for him
often he communed with
him; that he would send for
him to Jerusalem, A. 24, 25.
G. sent word and messengers
for her children,   dg. 200.
for this cause have I called
for you, to see you and
speak with you,   A. 28.
I know nothing of it, b. 387.
send him word.

cuirfid an grád folach ar iomad peacad.

charity shall cover a multitude of sins,   1 *Peter*, 4.

cuirid sé fonn orrainn ar maoin do roinn go fialmar ris na bochtaib.

it inclines us to share our goods freely with the poor,   *d*. 166.

cuirfead-sa a fuath air.

I will turn him against it.

furfaire do chur ar áit.

to blockade a place,   *b*. 75.

do chuir mé furtacht air.

I have helped him,   *ps*. 89.

ro chuir gairm ós árd orruib.

he loudly summoned them.   *dg*. 104.

geall churthar ar thalam nó ar maoin oile, neac chuireas geall ar ní ar bioth.

a mortgage which is put on land or other property ; one who mortgages any thing,   *b*. 473.

is olc na geasa do chuiris orm.

evil are the bonds under which thou hast laid me.   *dg*. 54.

ro chuir D. geasa orm gan aon laoch dá g-ceingeolad féin do sgaoilead dam.

D. has bound me not to loose any warrior whom he should bind,   *dg*. 54, 104.

cuir an glas ar an dorus.

lock the door,   *b*. 172.

do chuir glas air.

he locked it up,   *ob*. 433.

cuir glas ar dorus an phárlúis.

lock the parlour door.

do druid sé doirse an phárlúis air, agus do chuir glas orra.

he shut the doors of the parlour upon him, and locked them,   *Judges*, 3.

do chuir sé glas ar a thaisgid.

he locked his trunk,   *b*. 420.

cuirid sé an gloine deallrach ar do súilib.

he plays the dazzling glass in your eyes,   *b*. 393.

mórdacht agus glóir do chuir tú air.

majesty and glory thou hast laid upon him,   *ps*.

cuirid sí an gníom ortsa.

she attributes it to you, *b*. 398.

gluais do chur ar an sgríbinn diada ; do chur gluaise air.

to expound the Scripture ; to comment on it, *b*. 201, 126.

gnúis maith do chur ar droch-luimthe.

to put a good face on a bad game,   *b*. 204.

gruaim do chur ar a maillíde.

to knit his brows,   *b*. 386.

iargnó do chur go fios dóib ar an Spiorad Naom.

to consciously grieve the Holy Ghost.

ní chuirid focail breága ím ar meacanaib.

fair words butter no parsnips,   *b*. 205.

do chuireadar impíde air go
m-bainfidís le h-imeal a
eudaig amáin ; do maith
mé na fiacha úd uile duit,
do bríg gur chuir tú impíde
orm.

they besought him that they
might touch merely the
hem of his garment ; I
forgave thee all these debts,
because thou desiredst me,
m. 14, 18.

do chuireadar impíde air.

they besought him, *A.* 25.

do chuir phairisíneach áirige
impíde air a dinnér do
chaitheam na fochair.

a certain pharisee besought
him to dine with him, *l.* 11.

d'iarraid uirre impíde do chur
air.

asking her to beseech him,
s. 2.

do chuireadar iomrám treun,
tinneasnach ar an luing.

they rowed the ship strongly
and mightily, *dg.* 162.

na cumachta do chuir Dia ar
a ionntaob.

the power with which God has
entrusted him, *b.* 370.

cuirid tú iongnad orm, má's
ormsa labrann tú mar so.

you astonish me, if it is of me
you speak in this manner.

níor chuir sé irial orm.

he did not give a reply to me,
ob. 309.

an té chuireas a lám ar
sgríbinn.

he who puts his hand to a
writing (who subscribes it),
b. 499.

cuirid sí a láma ar an maide
sníomtha.

she puts her hands to the
spindle.

cuir do lám uirre agus biaid sí
beó.

lay thy hand on her and she
shall live, *m.* 9.

o. do chuir siadsan a láma
annsan.

they laid their hands upon
.him (to take him), *mk.* 6.

cuirimid anam ar m-bráthar
dílis ar do lámaib-sé.

we commend the soul of our
dear brother into thy hands.

o. do chuireamair-ne lám
ann.

we took him, *A.* 24

o. do luide sé lám throm air
féin

he laid violent hands upon
himself, *b.* 398.

gíd b'é neach chuireas a lám
ar an g-ceucht agus feuchas
'na díaig, ní b-fuil sé iomchubaid do ríogacht Dé.

who ever puts his hand to the
plough and looks back, is
not fit for the Kingdom of
God, *l.* 9.

an tan chuireas Dia leathtrom
orm.

when God afflicts me with
crosses, *d.* 372.

luach nó meas do chur ar ní.

to price or estimate a thing,
b. 195.

luathġáir do chur air; cuirid sé luathġáir ar mo chroíde.

to make him glad; it gladdens my heart, *b.* 260, 374.

do chuireadar luathġáir mór ar na bráithrib uile.

they caused great joy unto all the brethren, *A.* 15.

creid mé go g-cuireann sé luathġáir mór orm.

believe me that it gives me great pleasure.

cuirid sé lúthġáir chroíde orm d'fáicsin cómaith sin.

it gladdens my heart to see you so well, *b.* 374.

do chuir sé luathġáire ar an othar ar aisioc a sláinte.

he congratulated the patient on the recovery of his health.

cuirid siad luíġeachán ar a b-fuil féin.

they lay wait for their own blood, *pr.* 1.

ar g-cur luiġeacháin ar an t-sliġe fá chómair a marbtha.

laying wait in the way to kill him, *A.* 25.

do hinnisead damsa gur mian riu luíġeachán do chur air; ag cur luiġeacháin do na Iudaidib air.

I was told that they meant to lie in wait for him; when the Jews laid wait for him,
A. 23, 20.

mabail do chur air; ní cailltear gach ní ar a g-curthar maill; malairt gné do chur air féin.

to put a sham upon him; all is not lost that is delayed; to put on a new face,
b. 604, 426, 492.

do chuir tú maill fada orm; cuiread sin moill rófad orruinn.

you made me stay a long while; that would delay us too long.

do chur ar neach mairtíreacht d'fulang.

to make one suffer martyrdom,
b. 447.

meadrad do chur air.

to make mirth of him, *b.* 248.

mearúġad do chur air; do chur mearuiġthe ar ní lé foclaib dosġúdacha.

to non-plus him; to use chicanery about a thing,
b. 113, 497.

cuir meisneach air.

encourage him, *ob.* 347.

do chur misniġ air.

to exhort him, *b.* 200.

o. thuġais meisneach dam.

thou hast comforted me,
ps. 86.

mímhisneach do chur air.

to dispirit him, to cast him down, *b.* 167, 106.

miangus do chur ar a íoldúil.

to set his curiosity agog, *b.* 20.

cuirid sé milleun ormsa tré brisead ar g-cáirdis; ní feudaim a milleun do chur ortsa; milleun do chur air.

he blames me for the breach of our friendship; I cannot blame you for it; to cast the fault on him, *b.* 72, 106.

ní chuirfead milleun ag F. orruibse.

I will not cause F. to be angry with you, *dg.* 70.

mímisneach do chur air.

to dispirit him, *b.* 167.

do chuir sin meanma ar an mórsollaṁuin-se.

that gave life to the great solemnity, *b.* 410.

do chur míochoṁgair air.

to incommode him, *b.* 165.

míosásaṁ do chur air.

to molest him, *b.* 469.

ó so amach na cuiread aon duine míosuaiṁneas ormsa.

from henceforth let no man trouble me, *Gal.* 6.

ré g-curthaoi mísuaiṁneas ar na hollaṁnaib.

by which the learned were discouraged, *k.*

ná cuirthear míosuaiṁneas air.

let him not be disturbed.

tugadar fíon air ar cuiread mirr ré n-a ól dó.

they gave him to drink wine mingled with myrrh, *mk.* 15.

d'eagla go g-cuirfide moill ar bith air annsa n-Asia.

lest he should be detained in Asia, *A.* 20.

ní do chur a muda air.

to bereave him of a thing, *b.* 64.

móid do chur air.

to administer an oath to him, *b.* 259.

nach ar hollṁuiġead chum muirígne do chur ar an meaṁair.

which are not intended for charging the memory, *d.* xxv.

mórchoir do chur air.

to call him in question for his life, *b.* 410.

náire do chur air; cuirid sé náire orm.

to put him to shame; he makes me ashamed, *b.* 39, 77.

d'eagla go g-cuirfead sé náire ort.

lest he put thee to shame, *pr.* 25.

o. do náiriġ tú iad do bríġ gur diúlt Dia iad.

thou hast put them to confusion because God hath despised them, *ps.* 53.

cuir ola ar do cheann.

anoint thy face, *m.* 6.

fear bréige chum oṁain do chur ar eunlaith, oṁan do chur air.

a scare-crow to frighten birds; to startle him, *b.* 450, 622.

n'íl cuṁachta agad orduġaḋ do chur orm ; orduġaḋ do chur ar chúrum.

you have no power to command me; to manage a business, *b.* 125, 443.

peann do chur ar pháipeur.

to put pen to paper, *b.* 531

peannaid do chur air.

to inflict punishment on him, *b.* 357.

peurfum do chur ar ní.

to perfume a thing, *b.* 109.

cuirid tú iomad péine orm.

you put me to much pain, *b.* 253.

pláiġe do chur air ; a Dé ! do chuir pláiġe ar do phobul féin.

to plague him ; O God, who didst send plague upon thy people.

do chuir sé plána air.

he gave it a plausible colour, *oḃ.* 387.

púicín do chur air.

to hoodwink him, *b.* 320.

cuir ráth orra lé gach uile ṡonas.

prosper thou them with every happiness.

an ruaig do chur air ; ruaig do chur ar náṁaid ; d'obair go g-curthaoi an ruaig ar an rann clí don t-sluaġ.

to put him to the run ; to discomfit the enemy ; the left wing had like to have been routed, *b.* 413, 165, 589.

na sála do chur a n-áirde air.

to trip up his heels, *b.* 306.

do chonnairc sé iadsan ag cur saothair ṁoir orra féin ag iomraṁ, óir doḃí an ġaoth 'nan aġaiḋ.

he saw them toiling in rowing ; for the wind was contrary to them, *mk.* 6.

nó go g-cuirfeam seula ar ṡearboġantaiġiḃ ár n-Dé a g-cláraiḃ a n-eudan.

till we shall seal the servants of our Lord in their foreheads, *Apoc.* 7.

an té chuireas seachrán ar an dall as a ṡlíġe.

whoso maketh the blind to go out of his way, *Deuteron.* 27

do chuir sé seile ar an talaṁ.

he spat upon the ground.

gach sgél d'á g-cuireann sé síos ar an b-féin.

every tale which he sets down concerning the Fian, *K.* lxiv.

do chuir sé sgeula orruinn.

he sent for us, *dg.* 82.

do chuir sé sgían ar a sgórnaiġ.

he held the dagger to his throat, *b.* 317.

cuirid eaglaisiḋe na h-Asia beatha agus sláinte chugaiḃ.

the churches of Asia salute you, 1 *Cor.* 16.

slán do chur leis ; slán oídche
do chur ris.
do chuir sí sliocht air.
is biad agas deoch dó so,
.i. cuirfead aníd-se sólás mór
air.
do chuir mé sólás air do beith
fá míseun ; sólas croíde do
chur air.
do chuir sé sólás ar mo
chroíde ; cuirfidear sólás
orra.
do bríg gur córa dib sólás do
chur air ; má chuirim-se
doilgeas oraibse cia hé
chuireas sólás orm féin?
do réir mar do chuir Dia
sonas air.
cuir sparn ort.

sraith do chur air.
doh féidir sult do chur ar
éinneach.
cuir-si techta ar a chenn.
taithíge do chur air.

cíd b'é ar bith fá'r cuiread an
tinneas so ort.

do chuir sé é 'na thigearna ar a
thig.
do chuir sé tinól agus tiomsúgad orraib ar aon láthair.
ro chuir sé tiomsúgad ar seacht
g-cathaib.

do chuir sé tógairm ar churad-
aib.
cuirfid mé tnúth orraib lé
cinead nach b-fuil 'na
chinead, le cinead míothuí-

to bid him farewell; to bid
him good night, *b.* 69.
she bore him children, *K.* cii.
this is food and drink to him,
i.e., this thing would give
him great comfort. *b.* 453.
I comforted him on his misfortune ; to gladden his
heart, *b.* 518, 303.
it gladdened my heart; they
shall be comforted.

because ye ought rather comfort him ; if I make you
sorry, who is he that makes
me glad ? *2 Cor.* 2.
as God hath prospered him,
1 Cor. 16.
do your utmost, your worst,
ob. 449.
to fine him, *b.* 217.
a jest may be played on anyone, *b.* 507.
send messengers to him.
to pick an acquaintance with
him, *b.* 536.
for what cause soever this
sickness has been sent to
you.
he made him lord of his house,
ps. 105.
he caused them to be as-
sembled and collected in
one spot, *dg.* 142.
he made a muster of five
battalions, *dg.* 206.
he summoned champions,
ob. 479.
I will provoke you to jealousy
by them that are no people,
and I will make you angry

D

gseach cuirfid mé fearg orraib ; chum tnútha do chur orrasan.

cia hé misi do feudfad toirmeasg do chur ar Dhia?

ná cuir toirmeasg ar grásaib d'fágail don marb.

toirmeasg curthar ar níd.

do cuiread toirmeasg orm go minic fa theacht chugaibsi.

ní chuirfead-sa toirmeasg air ; toirmeasg do chur ar a sólás ; toirmeasg do chur ar neach atá ag labairt ; cuirid sin toirmeasg orm.

ní gabann sé féin na dearbráithre chuige, agus cuirid toirmeasg ar an druing lé'r mian.

an toirmeasg do chuirid ar leathnúgad an chreidim.

do chuireamar toirmeasg air ar son nách leanann sé sinn.

ag sírim ar Dhia gan a ainnéis féin do chur toirmisg ar thíodlaicídib Ríg na féile.

cruadchás do chuirfead toirmeasg ar gníomugad na haisdeoireachta.

cuirfe mé tómus anois orruib.

cuirid tóruigeacht orra go luath, óir beurthaoi orra.

do chuireadar troid orm.

ionnus nach g-c uirfinn ró-ualach oruibse uile.

with a foolish nation ; to provoke them to jealousy,
Rom. 10. 11.

what am I that I could withstand God?   A. 11.

prevent not the dead man from finding grace, s. 110.

an obstacle which is put to a thing,   b. 506.

I have been often hindered from coming to you,
Rom. 15.

I will be no hindrance to him ; to disturb his joy ; to disturb one who is speaking ; that disturbs me,
b. 314, 168.

he does not himself receive the brethren and forbids them that would,
3rd Epist. of St. John.

the obstacle they put to the propagation of the faith.

we forbade him because he followed not us,   mk. 9.

beseeching God that his own unworthiness may not stop the effects of the divine bounty.

a difficulty which might obstruct the action of the play,   b. 506.

I will now give you a riddle,
Judges, 14.

pursue them quickly, for ye shall overtake them,
Joshua, 20.

they induced, forced me to fight.

that I may not overcharge you all,   2 Cor. 2.

do chuir sé uathbás orm.

do chuireadar uathbás or-
ruinn.

mná áirige dínn féin do chuireadar uathbás orruiun.

ag cur soluis mar eudach ort.

cuir ort; bí mé uair nó dó ar
tí cur orm.

cuir do baireud nuad ort.

do aithin sé díob a m-bróga
do chur orra agus gan dá
chóta do beith iompa.

cuir órtsa do bhróga.

do chuireas mo brat orm.

o. cuir do brat umad, cuir do
chrios thort, agus ceangail
ort do bróga.

tabraid an chulaid sin is feárr
lib agus cuirid uime í; agus
cuirid fáinne ar a láim agus
bróga ar a chosaib.

do chur a chasóige air.

o. do chur a chasóige uime.

cuir do chrios ort agus friotháil ormsa.

do chuir asal croiceann leoin
air.

cuir dobáil pice air.

do chuir sé a airm agus a
éidead air.

cuir ort t'éide.

ag cur a chuid eudaig air.

cuir do chuid eudaig ort.

tar éis do chuid eudaig do
beith ort.

eudach do chur ar leanb.

ba chóir duit eudach olla do
chur air.

cuir ort do hata.

it amazed me,   b. 27.

they made us astonished,
                                l. 24.

certain women of our company
made us astonished,   l. 24.

decking thyself with light as it
were with a garment,
                              ps. 104.

dress yourself; I was once or
twice about to dress.

put on your new cap.

he commanded them to be
shod with sandals and not
put on two coats,   mk. 6.

put your shoes on.

I put on my coat,   b. 513

cast thy garment about thee,
gird thyself and bind on
thy sandals,   A. 12

bring forth the best robe and
put it on him; and put a
ring on his hand and shoes
on his feet,   l. 15.

to put on his coat,   b. 122.

gird thyself and serve me,
                                l. 17.

an ass put on a lion's skin.

daub it with pitch.

he put on his arms and
armour,   dg. 128.

put on your armour,   ob. 216.

putting on his clothes, d. 404.

dress yourself.

when you are dressed.

to dress a child,   b. 174.

you should apply flannel to it.

put on your hat.

cuir do léine ġlan ort féin.
put on your clean shirt.

o. boinn do chur fá phéire sto-cuíde.
to put vamps on a pair of stockings, *b.* 227.

o. do chuireadar brat purpuir uime.
they put a purple robe on him.

o, do chur a chóta uime.
to put on his coat, *b.* 225.

o. creud chuirfeam umainn?
wherewithal shall we be clothed?

o. nábídid lán do chúram creud chuirfid umaib.
be not solicitous about what ye shall put on, *m.* 6.

o. an ṁuintir chuireas eudaiġe míne iompa.
those that wear soft clothing *m.* 11.

o. do bí mé lomnocht agus do chuireabair-si eudach umam.
I was naked and ye clothed me, *m.* 25.

neaṁṁarbacht do ġabáil uime.
to put on immortality.

cuiream iomainn éidead an t-soluis; cuirid iomaib an Tiġearna Iosa Críosd.
let us put on the armour of light; put ye on the Lord Jesus Christ, *Rom.* 13.

ar g-cur éidiġ uchta na fíreuntachta iomaib agus bróga ulṁaiġthe Shoisgéil na síothchána fá bur g-cosaib.
having on the breastplate of righteousness, and your feet shod with this preparation of the gospel of peace,
Ephes. 6.

Deunaim, Do ġhním, I do.

deunam ar an taob úd anunn don loch.
let us go over to the other side of the lake, *b.* 8.

do deunaṁ ar aġaid ar neach.
to make towards one, *b.* 441.

do ṁothuiġeas iomad fear ag deunaṁ orm; do ṁothuiġeas iomad soiġdiuiríde ag deunad orm; deun ar an árd deas, ann súd atá m' iomraiġtheoir-se ag deunad.
I perceived many men making towards me; I saw many soldiers making towards me; ply to the south, there my waterman plies, *b.* 441, 543.

deunaid róṁuib ar an n-dubaiġeun.
launch out into the deep, *l.* 5.

do deunfam slíġe eile ar na gnódthuide.
we will go another way to work, *b.* 264.

ní deunfainn ar mo bás é.
I would not do it if I were to die, *b.* 495.

deun-sa orra-sa mar do rignis ar Iabin ag abainn Císon.

táim ar mire chum deunaṁ air.

an lucht íbeas deoch láidir do rinneadar abrán ormsa.

deunaid sé agairt ar an saoġal a d-taob peacaid.

aiġneas do deunaṁ ar ní.

do níd ainleanṁuin ar an té do buail tusa.

deun-sa ainleanṁuin orra lé d' anfad.

do bríġ go n-déarna ainleanṁuin ar an n-duine m-bocht.

is ní sin ag a'r fíu duit h-aire agus do dícholl do deunaṁ timchioll air.

aireachus do deunad air.

o. cúrum do deunad dó.

tabair grása dúinn aithris do deunaṁ ar do Naoṁaib.

atá d'fiachaib orruinn aithris do deunaṁ air.

deun aithris ar an m-beachán binn.

aithris do deunad air ní; do deunaṁ aithrise air.

do bríġ go n-deunann sé aithris ar imirc Ch. as Egipt.

do ġním aṁrus ar a ṁacántacht.

do níd anchaint ar an lucht ag a b-fuil áirdcheannas.

an té nach dearna anchaint a n-aġaid na h-anchaintc do riġnead air.

anforlann do deunaṁ ar an b-pobul.

do thou unto them as unto Jabin at the brook of Cison.

my fingers itch to be at him,
    b. 377.

those who drink strong drink made a song against me,
    ps. 69.

he will reprove the world of sin.

to discourse or dispute a thing
    b. 165, 355.

they persecute him whom thou hast smitten,   *ps.* 69.

persecute them with thy tempest,   *ps.* 83.

because he persecuted the poor man,   *ps.* 109.

this is a thing worth your employing your best care and pains about,   *b.* 346.

to look to him,   *b.* 424.

to look to him,   *b.* 424.

give us the grace to imitate thy saints.

we are bound to imitate him.

take example by the melodious little bee.

to imitate a thing; to imitate him,   *b.* 342, 343.

because it gives an account of C.'s journey out of Egypt.

1 doubt of his honesty.

they speak evil of dignitaries,
    Jude 1.

who when he was reviled, reviled not again,   1 *Peter* 2.

to devour the people,   *b.* 161.

árachas do deunaṁ ar ní.

to insure a thing, *b.* 365.

do gníd sé árdúgad ar na fíogracha.

it raises the figures, *b.* 501.

ármach do deunad ar an námuid.

to slaughter the enemy, *b.* 480.

ní do gníd at suas ar an arán.

a thing that makes bread swell up, *b.* 214.

do rinnead atharach ar neithib; a n-áit a n-déarnad atharach ar neithib do bunáitiġead go hormuisneach.

a change has been made of things; where a change hath been made of things advisedly established.

athchuiṁne do deunaṁ ar ní san meabair.

to refresh the memory of a thing in the mind.

do rinne Florus athchumaireacht ar an stair Róṁánaiġ.

Florus made an epitome of Roman history, *b.* 193.

ar n-deunaṁ bagair orra dó do aithin sé díob.

he straightly charged them and commanded them, *l.* 9.

do deurad bagair ar neach oile.

to huff another person, *b.* 328.

oud holc an beart do rinne sé ort.

bad was the deed, or turn, he did to you.

beathaiġiġ allta re fiadach do deunaṁ orra.

to make game of them.

deun breitheaṁnas orm agus tagair mo chúis; deuntar breitheaṁnas ar na geintib ad' radarc; do ġeuna sé breitheaṁnas ar an talaṁ ré fíreuntacht.

judge me and defend my cause; let the heathen be judged in thy sight; he shall judge the world with righteousness, *ps* 43, 9.

ar suideann tú do deunad breitheaṁnais ormsa do réir an dliġid?

sittest thou to judge me, according to the law?
     A. 23.

c um breitheaṁnais do deunaṁ ar an n dílleachta agus ar an té fóiréiġeantar.

to render justice to the orphan and the oppressed. *ps.* 11.

is ró beag mo ṡuim a m-breitheaṁnus do deunad daoibse orm; acht fós ní beirim breath orm féin; is é an Tiġearna an tí is breitheaṁ orm.

I care very little of the judgment which may be formed of me by you, yet I judge not my own self; it is the Lord that is my judge,
     1 *Cor.* 4.

atá se ag teacht do deunaṁ breitheaṁnais ar an d-talaṁ; do ḃeura sé breith ar an t-saoġal.

he cometh to judge the earth; he will judge the world, *ps.* 96.

ꝰ. corob é caemna dorónsat for na biastaib.

and it was the remedy they made against the reptiles.

o. d'a g-caoṁna ar ḋilinn.

to protect them from the deluge, *b.* 224.

cáinead do ḋeunaṁ air.

to jeer or jibe at him.

laiḃeoraid ar ġlóir do ríoġach-ta, agus do ḋeunaid caint ar do neart.

they shall speak of the glory of the Kingdom, and shall talk of thy power, *ps.* 145.

mórán cainnte do ḋeunaṁ ar ḃeagán áḋbair.

to make many words about a trifle, *b.* 440.

carṫhanacht do ḋeunaṁ air.

to bestow charity on him, *b.* 66.

do ṡeasadar ag deunaḋ casa-oide air; do rinneaḋ casa-oid ris air gur díombáil sé a ṁaoin.

they stood accusing him; he was accused unto him that he had wasted his goods, *b.* 23, 16.

ná deun casaoid ar ṡeirḃíseach lé n-a ṁaiġistir.

do not accuse a servant to his master, *pr.* 30.

ná measuiġid go n-deuna mise casaoid orruibse leis an Aṫ-air (nó ag an Athair.)

think not that I will accuse you to the Father, *Gospel.*

deuntaoi casaoid orra le n-a m-bráṫhair.

they were accused to (or by) their brother.

o. ag casaoid liom.

'remonstrating to me', *ob.* 85.

o. tug sé d'a uide gurab cealg do rínne sí chugtha.

he thought in his mind that it was treachery she prac-tised towards them, *L.* 23.

ní deunfainn ar cheannach ar bioth é.

I would not do it for ever so much, *b.* 492.

do ḋeunaḋ ceasachta ar Dhia; dranntánuiḋ, neach do ġníd ceasacht ar an uile níd.

to murmur against God; a mutterer, one who murmurs at everything, *b.* 480, 482.

an Tiġearna do ġeunas claoch-lóḋ ar ar g-corp díbliġe.

the Lord who shall change our vile body.

cliothṁagad do deunaṁ air.

to flirt or jest at him, *b.* 224.

clodaireacht do ḋeunaṁ air.

to mump him, *b.* 479.

is ar a choṁairle doronad.

it is by his counsel it was done.

congbáil daingean do deunaṁ ar dóthchus na beatha.

to hold fast to the hope of life.

do rinneadar crannchur air.

they cast lots for it, *ob*. 134.

a Dhé, do rinne creacha orruinn, fá'r b-peacaidib !

O God, who hast wounded us for our sins !

creud do rinneadar na daoinesi ort, as a d-tug tú a choṁmór so do pheacad orra ?

what did this people to thee that thou hast brought so great a sin on them ? *ex*. 32.

ní biaid eagla orm creud do deunas feoil orm.

I will not fear what flesh can do unto me, *ps*. 56.

ní raib uain aige ar chuartúgad do deunaṁ ar ṡeanchus na críche-si air ar ġab do láiṁ scríobad.

he had not leisure to examine the antiquities of the country on which he undertook to write, *k*. liv.

ar do ġníoṁarthaib do deunad cuiṁne.

my talking shall be of thy doings, *ps*. 77.

cuiṁniġiuġad ṡollamanta do deunaṁ ar naoṁ.

to make commemoration of a saint, *b*. 126.

is ar do chuisil doronad.

it was by your advice it was done.

cuntus do deunaṁ ar a thursgán ; cunntus do deunaṁ ar ṡluaġ.

to make an inventory of his goods ; to review an army, *b*. 361, 589.

doġním dánacht oruib an tan nach bím bur láthair ; is mór an dánacht lábairt do ġním oruib.

when I am not in your presence I am bold towards you ; great is my boldness of speech towards you, 2 *Cor*. 7, 10.

níór beag an daonacht do rinneadar na daoine barbartha orruinn.

the barbarous people showed us no little kindness, *A*. 28.

ar thí díbfeirge do deunaṁ ormsa.

with intent to rebel against me, *dg*. 206.

do ġníd dídean don bocht ar an g-cloídeaṁ.

he saveth the poor from the sword, *Job*. 5.

díleaġad do deunaṁ orra.

to digest them, *k*. 46.

do deunaṁ díoġaltais ar na geintib, smachtuiġthe ar na daoinib.

to be avenged of the heathen, and to rebuke the people, *ps*. 149.

ag deunaṁ díogaltais ar a n-aindliġthib

punishing their transgressions, *ps*. 99.

ná deun díogaltas orruinn fá'r b-peacaidib.

do rinne sé díogaltus air.

o. do bain sé díogaltas de.

do deunaid mé díogaltus air.

do móidig go n-dígeolad ar Dhiarmaid gach a n-dearna air.

gidead fós do gní sib féin eugcóir agus díogbáil agus sin ar bur n-dearbráithrib

o. ar son na díogbála do rinnead dúinn.

o. do rinne sé díogbáil do maoin nó do chlú na comarsan.

gan díogbáil ar bith do deunam dó.

creud fá n-deuntar an díombáil sin ar an ola?

ní lámfar díth, dochar iná díogbáil do deunam ort.

do gníd sé a díthchioll ar mise do millead.

ar n-deunam an uile díthchill dam ar sgríobad chugaib a d-timcheall an t-slánuigthe choitchinn.

ag deunam dithchíll ar aondacht na spioraide do choimeud a g-coim-cheangal síothchána.

muna n-deunam dá rírib ar n-díthchioll ar an g-cuid is tábachtuige don dligeadh do chóimlíonad.

má níd féin díthchioll ar síothcháin do deunam ris; muna n-deunmaoid ar n-díthchioll ar sásad de thabairt do Dhia.

do not take vengeance on us for our sins.

he took his revenge on him.

he took vengeance on him.

I'll pay him off, *b.* 531.

he vowed that he would avenge on Diarmat all that he did against him, *dg.* 162.

nay, but ye yourselves do wrong and defraud, and to your brethren, 1. *Cor.* 6.

for the damage he did to us, *d.* 376.

he injured his neighbour's goods or reputation, *d.* 296.

without doing him any hurt, *l.* 4.

why was this waste of the ointment made? *mk.* 14.

none will dare to do thee harm, hurt, or damage, *dg.* 70.

he endeavours to undo me, *b.* 353.

when I gave all diligence to write unto you of the common salvation, *Jude* 1.

endeavouring to keep the unity of spirit in the bond of peace, *Ephes.* 4.

if we do not seriously endeavour to fulfill the most important part of the law.

if they do their endeavour to make peace with him; unless we use our endeavour to satisfy God, *d.* 200, 300.

do gníd sé díthchioll ar an uile duine do sásaṁ.

he studies to please every body.

deunam, díthchioll gnáthach ar deunaṁ do réir a orduiġthead.

let us make a constant endeavour to do as he commands, *b.* 134.

do rinnead díthchioll ar foclaiḃ cóiṁideacha do seachnad.

an endeavour was made to avoid foreign expressions, *d.* xxii.

do deunaid sé díchioll ar a chur fá deara daṁsa a deanaṁ.

he will go near to have me do it, *b.* 488.

deunam díthchioll ar ar saoirse anallód do thabairt tar ais nó do athrochtain.

let us endeavour to recover our former liberty, *b.* 230.

do gní an diabal dícheall ar a thoirmeasg.

the devil endeavours to hinder it, *s.* 65.

o. do gnid sé díthchioll re dul tar ais.

he makes an effort to go back, *b.* 186.

ní deunaid doiliġ ort.

it will do you no harm

droichní do deunaṁ air.

to disoblige him, *b.* 166.

do rinne sé dúnṁarbad air.

he killed him in cold blood, *b.* 75.

don eascaine sin dorónsat for C.

for that curse which they gave to C.

cia b'é háit a n-déarna éigceart ar aon duine.

wherever he has done wrong to any man.

má gní aoín neach éiliuġad agus foillsiuġad ar aon chol.

if any man do allege and discover any impediment.

do dén-sa éirleach agus athchumad ortsa féin agus ar do ṁuintir.

I will work slaughter and discomfiture on you and on your people, *dg.* 152.

o. noch do gnid eolus don lucht fairrge.

which guides mariners, *b.* 149.

ag iarraid fuirre ernaiġthe do d ṁnaṁ fuirre fris an choimdd d'á furtacht.

to ask her to pray for her to the Lord to help her, *fa.* 32.

ní déarnamar eudáil ar aon duine; a n-dearna mé eudáil oruiḃ a d-taoiḃ aonduine d'ar chuir mé chugaiḃ?

we have not defrauded any man; did I make a gain of you by any of them whom I sent to you, 2 *Cor.* 7. 12.

eugcóir ós cionn gach eugcóra, eugcóir do deunaṁ ar
duine ṁaith.

smuainid lib féin cad é mheud
na heugcóra do nísib ar Dhia.

níor fulaing sé d'aon duine
eugcóir do deunaṁ air.

ní déarnaiġ mé a beag d'eugcóir air.

a chompánaiġ ní b-fuilim ag
deunaṁ eugcóra ortsa, ané
nár réidiġ tú riom ar
phiġin ?

má riġne mé eugcóir ar aon
duine aisicim a cheithre
uiread.

an drong do ġníd faílliġe ar
theacht do láthair.

o. do thab irt faílliġe an
a chúram.

faire do deunaṁ air.

ag deunad faire oídche ar a
d-treud.

do deunaṁ feadaoile air.

ní dén feall air.

adeir C. go n-dearnadar
Brethnaiġ feall ar uacht-
aránaib na Roṁánach ; re
feall do deunaṁ ar chloinn
Uisnich ar foráiliom Ch.

gan feall fíorġrána mar so do
ġeunaṁ orm.

do níd feall ar an n-dilleacáta.

ollaṁ re ᴜᴄunaṁ feille ar a
chéile

cóṁnaiġ annsa Tiġearna agus
deur, feitheaṁ foiġideach
air · deunad Israel feitheam
air.

an injustice beyond every
injustice is to wrong a good
man,   *pr.*

consider with yourselves how
great an injury ye do to God.

he suffered no man to do him
wrong,   *ps.* 105.

I have not wronged him in
the least,   *b.* 402.

friend, I do thee no wrong ;
didst thou not agree with
me for a penny ?

if I have done wrong to any
man, I restore him fourfold,
      l. 19

those who fail to come,
      b. 499.

to neglect his duty, *d.* 490.

to look to him,   *b.* 424.

keeping night-watch over their
flock,   *l.* 2.

to hiss him,   *b.* 315.

I will do him no treachery,
      dg. 92.

C. says that the Britons mur-
dered the chief of the
Romans ; to murder the children of Usnech at the instigation of C.,   *k.* xii, 372.

not to do me such foul treachery,   *dg.* 190

they put the fatherless to death,
      ps. 94.

ready to murder each other,
      k. xxii.

hold thee still in the Lord and
abide patiently upon him ;
let Israel trust in him,
      ps. 37, 131.

do rinne sé fiadach ar ġeirrḟiaiġ.

he hunted a hare,   *b.* 331.

an té do ġníd fiadach . ar eunlaith.

he who hunts birds,   *b.* 234.

beathaiġiġ allta **ré** fiadach do deunaṁ orra.

wild animals to be hunted.

fiaġach do deunad ar ġeirrḟiaiġ nó ar ṡionnach.

to hunt a hare or fox,   *b.* 331.
                         b. 246.

do deuna sí fiadach ar an m-beatha ṁórluaiġ.

she will hunt for the precious life,   *pr.* 5.

do ġním fiadnuise air.

I testify to it.

o. do ġní sé fiadnuise liom.

He beareth witness of me, *j.* 8.

tré nach raib riachtanus aige lé duine ar bith do deunaṁ fiadnuise ar duine.

because he needed not that any one should bear witness of man.

o atá tú ag deunaṁ fiadnuisse duit féin; *o.* an té d'a n-déarna tú fiadnuise.

you bear record of yourself; the person to whom thou hast borne witness.

fionġal do deunaṁ orra.

to murder them,   *Lir.* 14.

do rinne sé fiosrad ar droch-daoinib na háite.

he made inquiries about the bad people of the place.

). creud é mac an duine as a b-fiosruiġeann tú é.

what is the son of man that thou visitest him,   *ps.* 8.

do deuna sé fochṁaid orra.

he shall deride them,   *ps.* 2.

e. fochṁuide do deunaṁ fá chreidioṁ.

to deride religion,   *b.* 159.

o. gid bé fochṁaideas an bocht tarcuisniġid sé a cruthaiġtheoir.

whoso mocketh the poor reproacheth his Maker, *pr.* 17.

foillsiúġad reusúnta do deunad ar níd.

to make a reasonable demonstration of a thing,   *b.* 449.

atá foiréigean d'á · deunaṁ ar an ríoġacht neaṁda; ná deunaid foiréigean ar duine ar bith ; atá gach uile duine ag deunaṁ foiréigin air; ni deunaid an náṁaid foiréigean air.

the kingdom of heaven suffers violence ; do violence to no man ; every man doth violence to it ; the enemy shall not do him any violence,
        m. 11, *l.* 3, 16, *ps.* 89.

do bríġ go n-deunaid mórán foiréigean air.

because many do violence to him,   *d.* 368.

deunamaoid foiréigean orra.

let us oppress them.

an duine do ní foirneart ar
fuil duine ar bith teithfid sé
chum an phuill.
fonoṁad do deunam ar neach.
do rinne sé fonoṁad air.
o. do deunaṁ fonoṁaid
taoi.
o. cluiṁthe fonoṁaid do
deunaṁ dó ; do rinne sé
cloch rothnóis díoṁsa.
o. ná deuntar sgige a n-Dia.
o. do deuna sé gáire uime.

o. an t-súil do ní magaid fá
n-a athair.
do deunaṁ forbais for Eirinn.

do ronsat forbaisi for Sráith
Cluaide ocus for ṁuintir an
Tomrair sin.
ní léigfead duit fuiliuġad iná
foirdeargad do deunaṁ air.
fromad do deunaṁ ar ṡean-
chus Eironn.

is mar sin do rinn U. gabáltus
ar na Saxaib.
d'eagla go n-déindis gáirdeachas orm.
gairm tar ais do deunaṁ ar
cheachtar don dá breitheaṁnas.
éist inn an tan do nímid gairm
ort.
gairm phósda do deunaṁ ar
lánaṁain 'san eaglais.
ní ar a n-deunann A. gearán a
n-aimsir féin.
na peacaide áiriġe ag a n-
deunann a choinsíos gearán
air umpa.

a man that doth violence to the
blood of any person shall
flee to the pit, *pr.* 28.
to flout at a person, *b.* 223.
he played upon him, *b.* 541.
to make game of him (faoi *is
the usual preposition*), *b.* 223.
to make a laughing stock of
him ; he made a mocking
stock of me, *b.*
God is not mocked, *Galat.* 6.
he shall laugh him to scorn,
ps. 37
the eye that mocketh at his
father, *pr.* 30.
to make a conquest of Erinn,
ob. 256.
they laid siege to Strathclyde,
and to the people of that
Tomrar, *fa.* 192, 166.
I will not let you cut or
wound him, *dg.* 152.
to regulate the annals of
Ireland, *better*, to test them,
K. cxi.
it is thus W. made conquest of
the Saxons, *Keating*, xlviii.
lest they should triumph over
me, *ps.* 38,
to appeal from or revoke
either judgment, *d.* 186.

hear us when we call on thee,
ps. 20.
to bid the bans of matrimony,
b. 69.
a thing of which A. complains
in his own time.
the particular sins of which his
conscience accuses him.

gearán do deunaṁ a n-aġaid éigcirt.

to exclaim against injustice,
b. 199.

iarraim d'athchuinge orraib geurchoimeud do deunaṁ daoib ar an ṁuintir thógbas siosma.

I beseech you to be on your guard against those who cause schism, *Rom.* 16.

do níthear géirleanṁuin air.

he is persecuted, *d.* 236.

do ġní ríġ nua géirleanṁuin orra.

a new king sorely oppresses them, *ex.*

do ní an cionntach géirleanṁuin ar an m-bocht.

the sinner persecutes the poor, *ps.* 10.

d'eagla go n-deuntaoi géirleanṁuin orra.

lest they should be persecuted, *Galat.* 6.

noch fós do rinne géirleanṁuin orainne.

who also persecuted us,
1 *Thess.* 2.

gearuídacht do deunaṁ air.

to jeer at him, *b.* 244.

geurscrúdaḋ do deunaṁ ar rúindiaṁraib an chreidiṁ.

to pry into the mysteries of faith, *b.*

gid b'é gleus ar a n-deunfaid tú é.

what way soever you will do it, *b.* 328.

do deunaṁ glaṁsáin air.

to murmur against him, *b* 480.

dogní gnúisfilleaḋ ar an g-créatuir.

he turns his face to the creature, *s.* 56.

maisead déin grása orruinn an chuibreach do bogaḋ orruinn.

then do us the favour to slacken our bonds, *dg.* 138.

a n-áit an iothomráid do ġníd orraib.

whereas they speak against you, 1 *Peter*, 2.

do deunaḋ iomurca air.

to huff him, *b.* 328.

deunaid iudicecht air.

judge him, *ob.* 310.

do deuna mé iasgairiġe ar daoinib dib.

I will make you fishers of men,
Mat. 4.

glacaireacht nó láiṁsiugaḋ do deunaṁ air.

to touch or handle it.

ni ġníd rann acht lagugaḋ ar an duain airdchéimeach.

rhyme but weakens heroic verse, *b.* 189.

do rinneadar láṁach le piléir beaga orruinn.

they plied us with small shot, *b.*

deunaid siad láṁach amach ar a náṁuid.

they shoot out at their enemy,
b. 425.

cómartha chum lámaiġ do deunad air.

a mark to shoot at, *b.* +46.

leanṁuin do ġníthear ar choirioch do láthair.

a fresh prosecution which is carried on against a criminal, *b.* 237.

is í toil Dé gan leathtrom ná meabail do deunaṁ d'aoinneach ar a dearbráthair

this is the will of God that no man go beyond or defraud his brother.

cia nach saoilfead go n-déarnad leathtrom mór air?

who would not think that a great wrong was done to him?

leathtrom do deunaṁ air.

to deal cruelly with him, *d.* 182.

leithéis do deunaṁ air.

to pick a hole in his coat, *b.* 318.

gan luad nó imrád do deunaṁ orra.

without making mention of them, *k.* xcii.

magad do deunaṁ air.

to jeer at him, *b.* 337.

do deunair magad orra ; do deunair tarcuisne ar na cineadachaib uile.

thou shalt have them in derision ; thou shalt laugh all the heathen to scorn, *ps.* 59.

do ġníthear magad tarcuisneach ar an duine cheart díreach ; an áill lib magad do deunaṁ air-sion?

the just upright man is laughed to scorn ; would ye mock him? *Job.* 12, 13.

rinne maiġistir diob ar gach aoibneas.

he made them masters of every enjoyment.

an drong doġní maill ar thoil an ṁairb do chóiṁlíonad.

those who delay fulfilling the wish of the departed person. *s.* 130

fá ṁaith do deunaṁ orm féin.

for doing good to me, *dg.* 72.

do rinne sí obair ṁaith ormsa.

she hath done a good work on me, *mk.* 14.

a. a n-dorigeni Dia airriu de maith.

what good God did for them or to them.

a. cia dudrigni Dia mór di maith erriu.

though God hath done much of good for them.

creud is maith daṁsa do deunaṁ ar na geasaib úd.

what is good for me to do as to these bonds, *dg.* 58.

do ġním malairt ar áireaṁ bliadan.

I make a change in the number of years, *k.* cii.

ionnas gur lúġaide do deuntaoi malairt ar an seanchus é.

in order that there should be the less alteration in the history, *k.* cvii.

ná deunad aoinneach maoiṫ-feachas ar daonib.

let no man glory in men, 1 *Cor.* 3.

atâ an capall sin ar feabas ar a n-déarnad marcuiġeacht riaṁ.

that is as good a horse as ever was ridden, *b.* 66.

do beir tu orm marcuíġeacht do deunaṁ air.

thou causest me to ride upon it, *Job.* 30.

meabal do deunaṁ ort.

to do thee injury, *dg.* 154.

do iompoiġ sé a g-croíde chum meabla do deunaṁ orraib.

he turned their hearts to deal untruly with them, *ps.* 105.

is í toil Dé gan leathtrom ná meabail do deunaṁ d' éinneach ar a dearbráthair.

this is the will of God that no man go beyond and defraud his brother.

meuduġad do deunaṁ ?ʹ leabar.

to make an addition to a book, *b.* 13.

do thionnsgna ʹar mícheudfaid do deunaṁ air.

they began to be displeased with him, *mk.* 10.

milteanas do deunaṁ ar ní.

to blunder at or spoil a thing, *b.* 76.

milleun do deunaṁ ar ar g-creideaṁ.

to reprove our faith.

do rinneadar monbur air.

they murmured against him.

do deuna mé íasgaireada ar daoiṁb díb.

I will make you fishers of men, *mk.* 1.

gach mod ar a n-déarnamar é.

every way in which we did it, *d.* 284.

a ní atá ag a deunaṁ orm.

the thing which is done to me.

gach ní do deuna dóib mar ba vaith linn deunav dúinn féin ; agus gan aon ní do deunav orha nár vaith linn a deunav orrainn féin.

to do for them what we should like to be done for ourselves, and not to do anything against them that we should not like to be done against ourselves,

Cork Irish Catechism.

is iad Tuatha De Danann do ġní sin ortsa.

it is the Tuatha De Danann that are doing that to you, *dg.* 172.

a. móı ní as dénte ní airriu.

they must be made much of.

nó go d-tugaid díogal damsa ann gach níd d'á n-déarna sé orm.

a. hóre dorrigéni Crist an uile so errunn :

a. dorigéni Dia inso ar maccu Israel.

creud fá g-cuirthi buaidread uirre ? do rinne sé obair maith ormsa.

a. cid at móra na huilc dorónais frim.

ní deárna sé acht piocaireacht air.

ní deárna púdar ris an tarb.

do rinnead puiblideacht ar an d-tiottal ríoga.

ní gníd sé rún ar éin ní.

do chonnarc a samail aige dá deunam ar Chonán.

do rinneas sábáil maith air.

gabthaoi timcheall mara agus tíre do chum go n-deunad sib aon n-duine ar bur riagail.

do geuna urchóid sealg air.

do rinneabair sgige ar chómhairle an boicht.

ná deunaid olc a n-agaid uilc ar éinneach ; ná beiread an t-olc buaid oraib acht beiridse buaid ar an olc ré maith.

do rigne an ceard copair olc mór orm.

claoidtear na huaibrig óir do rinneadar olc orm gan ádbar.

na deuna olc ar bith duit féin.

until he give me satisfaction for every thing he has done to me, *dg.* 64.

though Christ hath done all that for us.

God did this for the children of Israel.

why trouble ye her ? she hath wrought a good work on me, *mk.* 14.

though great are the evils you have done me.

he did but nibble at it, *b.* 493.

it did no hurt to the bull, *ob.* 393.

the royal title was proclaimed.

he keeps no secret, *b.* 79.

I saw him do the like to Conan, *dg.* 122.

I made a good riddance of it, *b.* 581.

ye compass sea and land to make one proselyte, *m.* 23.

evil shall hunt him.

ye have made a mock of the counsel of the poor, *ps.* 14.

do not evil for evil to any man ; let not evil overcome you but overcome evil with good, *Rom.* 12.

the coppersmith did me much evil, 2 *Tim.* 4.

let the proud be confounded for they have done me evil without cause, *ps.* 119.

do thyself no harm, *A.* 16.

E

cia deunas olc orruib, má
leanann sib don ṁaith?

who will harm you if ye be
followers of that which is
good ?   1 *Peter*, 3.

o. do chualaiḋ mé ó ṁórán ar
an b-fear so a ṁeud d'olc do
rinne sé do na naoṁaib.

I have heard by many of this
man how much evil he hath
done to the saints,   *A.* 9.

o. dom ḟáidib ná deunaiḋ
dochar.

do my prophets no harm,
ps. 105.

do ḋeuna urchóiḋ sealg air
chum a ḋíbeartha.

evil shall hunt him to overthrow him,   *ps.* 140.

bíḋmar ag deunaṁ socruġad
ort.

we were speaking of you.

deunam stuideur ar ar léiġionn.

let us study our lesson.

do ḋeunaṁ stuidéir ar a
leabar.

to mind his book,   *b.* 80.

o. stuideuraiḋ croiḋe an
ionruic chum freagartha.

the heart of the righteous
studieth to answer, *pr.* 15.

do rinn mise an tairgsin ar a
n-dearnaḋ réiġteach go
coṁaontach.

I made the motion which was
unanimously agreed to,
b. 474.

go n-dearnadar tairngire ar
theacht Chríost.

and they made a prophecy of
the coming of Christ.

ar chroiḋe briste ní ḋeunair
tarcuisne ; do ḋeunair tarcuisne ar na cineaḋachaib.

thou shalt not despise a
broken heart ; thou shalt
laugh the heathen to scorn,
ps. 51, 59.

a Dhé nach deunann tarcuisne
ar csnaib chroiḋe choiṁ-
bruiġthe.

O God, who despisest not the
sighs of a broken heart.

o. do ḋeunainn tarcuisne dom'
beatha.

I would despise my life,
Job. 9.

an torṅaoideṁ do roinis orm.

the threat you have made to
me,   *fa.* 80.

do ġníd tóruiġeacht ar m'-
anam mar an n-gaoith.

they pursue my soul as the
wind,   *Job.* 30-

is sona an te do ní trócaire ar
na bochtaib.

happy is he that hath mercy
on the poor,   *pr.* 14.

deuna trócaire orm, atá m'
inġion ar n-a buaireaḋ.

have mercy on me, my
daughter is sorely vexed,
m. 15.

an é nár chóir duitsi trócaire do deunaṁ air aṁuil agus mar do rinne misi trócaire ortsa?

ag guide thú an trócaire cheudna-sain do deunaṁ do ġnáth orruinn.

deun trócaire orm a Dhia do réir do thrócaire móire.

deunaid trócaire orm, a lucht is caraid daṁ, óir do bean láṁ an Tiġearna riom.

o. an té onóruiġeas a Dhia bí trócaire ann don bocht.

do deunfa mé trócaire ar an té ar a n-deunfa mé trócaire, agus do deunfa mé truaiġe don té d'a n-deunaid mé truaiġe.

feuch-orm agus deun trócaire orm do réir do chleachtaid don druing lé'r b'ionṁain h-ainm.

o. taisbeunfad trócaire dó.

o. bí trócaireach daṁ a Dhé; go raiḃ Dia trócaireach dúinn.

o. deonuiġ trócaire dó.

gan do beith ag deunaṁ truim air.

nach déarnad truailead air ré fad aimsire.

tuarasġaḃáil chinnte do deunaṁ ar dúithche.

do deunfa sé uachtarántachtort.

do ġníd an biad so ualach ar mo ġoile.

o. do beith ar tí urchóide do deunad do neach oile.

shouldst thou not have had compassion on him even as I had pity on you? *m.* 18.

beseeching thee still to continue the same mercy to us.

have mercy on me, O God, according to thy great mercy. *ps.* 51.

have mercy on me O ye who are my friends, for the hand of the Lord hath touched me, *Job.* 19.

he that honours God hath mercy on the poor, *pr.* 14.

I will have mercy on whom I have mercy, and I will have compassion on whom I will have compassion, *Rom.* 9.

O look thou upon me and be merciful unto me, as thou usest to do unto those who love thy name.

I will show mercy to him, *ex.*

O God be merciful to us; God be merciful to us, *ps.* 56, 67.

grant him mercy, *b.* 175.

without your reviling him, *dg.* 122.

which has not been corrupted in the course of time.

to make an exact description of a country, *b,* 159.

he shall rule over thee, *Gen.* 3.

this meat oppress my stomach, *b.* 120.

to be about to do harm to another, *b.* 431.

Imirt, to play.

léigid do na críostaidib agus imrid for iodaladarthaib.

spare the Christians and strike the idolaters, *fa.* 182.

d'imirt ar chorr 's ar choinnlín.

to play at odd and even, *b.* 502, 196.

cluirathe do himearthar ar chárduíge.

a game which is played at cards, *b,* 392.

an cian ro clos gáir na b-fea og imirt diocumaing forra ; ased rá innisit go raba buairad mór for C. ar n-imirt driagachta do Thaircealtach fair.

far was heard the cry of men who were suffering discomfiture ; they tell that C. was in great trouble, Tairchealtach have exercised magic on him, *fa.* 136, 190.

béicedach na miled ag imirt éccomloinn orra.

the shrieks of the soldiers when they were being subdued, *fa.* 122.

geursúgrad d' imirt air.

to put a yoke upon him, *b.* 373.

teimeal báis d'o imirt air.

to execute the gloom of death on him, *dg.* 104.

d'imeirt ar chúpla 's ar chórr, d'imirt ar chórr is cuinniín ; d'imirt ar chorr 's ar choinnlín.

to play at odd and even ; to play at odd and even, *b.* 196, 508.

creud ar a n-imrim ?

what do I play for ?

creud ar a n-nimeoram ?

what shall we play for ?

d'imirt ar sáitéin ; d'imirt ar choisliáthróid.

to play at foils ; to play football, *b.* 225, 227.

agus iad ag imirt uirre.

and they playing on it (the chessboard).

ag imirt ar chláirsig.

playing on the harp.

ag imirt ar mailíde.

playing or fighting with cudgels, *b.* 145.

a. atetha a chlaideb do imbert fuiri.

he threatens to ply the sword on her.

sórt peannuide do himeathar ar lucht fairrge.

a kind of punishment inflicted on sailors, *b.* 170

dar imir droígiocht orruinn.

she practised druidism upon us, *Lir.* 44.

imeorad draoideacht air.

I will practise magic against him, *dg.* 166.

a. nela no mebul d'imirt dóib
for Tróianaib.
ag imirt fóirmirt orruinn.
ni mian leisan rig anthorlann
d'imirt ar a ógláoich ar chor
san m-bioth.
ionnus nach faicfidis do shúile
na huile olca imeórad ar an
ionad-so.

they offered insults and re-
proaches to the Trojans.
using violence to us. *a*. 253.
the king does not mean that
his subjects should be any
war oppressed. *h*. 10.
that your eyes may not see all
the evils I shall inflict on
this place. *c*. 170.

Tionnsgnadh, tosughadh, to begin.

tosdgad ar Dhia do grádugad.
má thoisigeann an t-aith-
rigeach ar Dia do grá-
dugad.
do thosuigeadar na daoine ar
meudugad ar druim na
talman.
do thosaig sé ar beith 'na
criadaire: do thosaig seision
beith 'na duine chúmacht-
ach ar an d-talam: do thoisi-
geadar so do deunam.
ag tionnsgnad ar Dhia do
ghrádugad.
atá an tinneas ag tionnsgnad
ar lagdugad.
ag tionnsgnad ar fás.
tionnsgnaid sé ar báisdig.
atá mo phian ag tionnsgnad ar
lagdugad.
tionnsgnaid sé ar baothchaint
do deunam.
e. thionnsgnadar beith go
súgach ; do thionnsgain sé
labairt.
c. do thionnsgain seisean
mallugad agus mionnugad.
ó'n g-ceud am a'r thosuigeadar
ar borrad suas.

to begin to love God. *i*. 230.
if the penitent begins to love
God. *i*. 278.
men began to multiply on the
face of the earth. *Gen*. 6.

he began to be a husbandman:
he began to be a mighty one
upon earth: they have
begun to do this.
Gen. 9. 10, 11.
beginning to love God.

the disease begins to abate.

beginning to grow.
it begins to rain. *h*. 60
my pain begins to abate. *d*. 2.

he begins to dote, *h*. 171.

they began to be merry: he
began to speak. *L* 15. 7.

he began to curse and swear,
ch. 14.
since first they began to spring
up, *a*.

o. do thionnsgnadar cúis do chur air.

they began to accuse Him, *l.* 23.

o. do thionnsgain sé teagasg do deunaṁ.

he began to teach, *mk.* 4.

o. tionnsgónaiḋ sé gabáil ar na buachaillidib.

he will begin to beat the boys, *l.* 12.

atá sé ag tionnsgnaḋ ar theacht chuṁ sláinte.

" he is beginning to revive "

do thosaiġ seision ar beith a riachtanus.

he began to be in want, *l.* 15.

tosúġaḋ Air a riar.

to begin to serve Him, *d.* xx.

tionnsgnaiḋ na caoire ar uain do breith.

the ewes begin to yean, *b.* 180.

o. atá sé ag tionnsgnaḋ seaca.

it begins to freeze, *b.* 236.

atá an t-síon ag tionnsgnaḋ ar ḋorchaḋ.

the weather begins to darken.

atá na reulta ag tionnsgnaḋ ar éirġe.

the stars are beginning to rise.

Glacaim, I take.

glacaiḋ mé orm í beith saor ó lochtaib.

I warrant her to be free from faults.

glacaiḋ sé mórán air féin san uile chuideachtain ; glacaiḋ sé a n-iomad air féin.

he assumes too much to himself in every society ; he arrogates too much to himself, *b.* 37, 42.

do ġlac sé uain ar a ḋeunaṁ 's gan mise do láthair.

he took the opportunity to do it in my absence, *b.* 6.

glac í ar earball.

take it by the tail, *ex.* 42.

do ġlac sé locht ormsa.

he took a disgust of me.

do ġlacaḋ ar cáirde.

to take upon tick, *b.* 166, 632.

nach nglacaḋ tú sgilin ar a b-fuil ann?

would you not take a shilling for what is in it?

ní raib sé ollaṁ ar aṁras ar bith do ġlacaḋ ar a cháirde.

he was not apt to entertain any suspicion of his friends, *b.* 192

cíos an ríġ do ġlacaḋ ar gabáltus.

to farm the king's revenues, *b.* 209.

conntus do ġlacaḋ ar fearaib an chablaiġ.

to take an account of the men of the navy, *b.* 487.

do ġlac sé fós ar ṁuineul mé.

he hath taken me by the neck,
Job , 16.

glacfaid an paintér é ar śáil agus beurfaid an sladṁóir air ; glacaid critheagal greim air.

the gin shall take him by the heel and the robber shall prevail against him ; terror takes hold of him, *Job.* 18, 27.

seilb do ġlacaḋ ar ar g-croíḋe.

to take possession of our heart.

Gabhaim, I take, betake myself, go.

do sguireadar do ġabáil air.

they ceased to beat him,
A. 21.

ar n-gabáil orra go róṁór ḋoiḃ ; tar éis gabáil orruinn go puiblide agus sinn neiṁchiontach.

when they had laid many stripes upon them; having beaten us publicly, though we were uncondemned,
A. 16.

do ġabadar air a ḃ-fiaḋnuisi chathaoireach an breitheaṁnais.

they beat him before the judgment seat, *A.* 18.

cuirfiḋ an breitheaṁ d'fiachaiḃ leagaḋ síos agus gabáil air d'a láthair féin, do réir a choire.

the judge shall cause him to lie down and to be beaten before his face, according to his fault,
Deuteron. xxv. 2.

do ġabadar na sgológa air ; ar n-gabáil airsion leis.

the husbandmen beat him ; having beaten him also,
l. 20.

gaḃ air, na gaḃ air.

beat him, don't beat him,
Scotch.

tionnsgónuiḋ sé gabáil ar na buaichilid agus na cailínid agus beith ar meisge.

he shall begin to beat the menservants and maids and to be drunk, *l.* 12.

geuḃthar mórán air ; buailfidear beagán air.

he shall be beaten with many stripes ; he shall be beaten with few stripes, *l.* 12.

do ġabadar orm agus níor ṁóthuiġ mé.

they have beaten me and I felt it not, *pr.* 23.

do gabad do ślataiḃ orm trí huaire, do gaṇaḋ orm aonuair do chlochaiḃ.

thrice was I beaten with rods, once was I stoned,
2 *Cor.* 11.

gabáil do śeilidio air; agus do ġabadar do basaib air.

dá n-iomchrad sib gabáil do dórnaib orraib.

fuair mé sgolb an m'feoil aingeal Shátáin chum gabála do dornuib orm.

do ġabadar do śeilidib a n-a eudan agus do ġabadar do basaib air.

a Iarusaléim ġabas do chlochaib ar an lucht chuirthear ad' ionsaiġe.

cia acu obair ar a son a n-gabthaoi do chlochaib orm.

O a Iarusaléim marbas na fáide agus ġabas do chlochaib ar na daoinib churthar chugad !

do ġab sé do chloich ar a cheann.

o. ragabad dóib do chlochaib.

d'iarradar siad gabáil do chlochaib ort.

chum iadsan do maslugad agus gabáil do chlochaib orra.

do ġabáil do chosaib air (nó ann).

gabaid an leoman d'a earball air féin.

geubaid do śeilidib air.

geubthar do śeilidib air.

do ġab sé do sgiúrsaib air.

do ġabadar dream eile do slataib air.

ro gabsat fair.

do gabadar ar chéle.

to spit on him ; and they struck him with the palms of their hands, *mk.* 14.

if ye should bear patiently to be buffeted, 1. *Peter*, 2.

I got a thorn in my flesh, the angel of Satan to buffet me, 2 *Cor.* 12.

they spit in his face and buffeted him, *m.* 26.

O Jerusalem that stonest them that are sent to thee, *m.* 23.

for which of these works do ye stone me ?

O Jerusalem, who killest the prophets and stonest them that are sent to thee ! *l.* 13.

he struck his head with a stone.

they were pelted with stones, *fa.* 146.

they sought to stone you.

to use them despitefully and to stone them, *A.* 14.

to kick him, *b.* 383.

the lion lashes himself with his tail. *s.* 72.

they shall spit upon him.

he shall be spitted upon, *m.* 10, *l.* 18.

he scourged him.

others smote Him with rods, *m.* 26.

they attacked him.

they attacked each other.

gebaid óin scol for aréli.

one school will attack or lash the other, *Wb.* 3.

ro ba Fionn ag gabáil do míslisbriathraib uirre.

Finn was plying her with sweet words, *dg.* 208.

do ġabáil for Athcliath.

to attack Dublin.

ro gabad dó do ġaib agus do thuaġaib.

he was attacked with javelins and axes, *fa.* 186.

o. do ġabáil do ġuaillib ann a chéile.

to jostle one another, *b.* 380.

o. ní choiglid gabáil do seilidib am' eudan.

they forbear not spitting in my face, *Job.* 428.

o. do ġab sé do sgin a n-a cheann.

he stabbed his head with a knife.

o. do ġabáil d'uilleannaib ann a chéile san g-cruinniúġad.

to elbow one another in the crowd, *b.* 331.

o. cor' buailset do slaitt hé i n-a chend.

and they struck him with a rod on the head.

ní gebmais uad.

we would not go or part from him, *fa.* 112.

ro ġabsat for a diubargan.

they continued to shoot at it, *fa.* 186.

do ġabsat ar eitiollach.

they took to flight, *Lir.*

is failliġtheach do ġabaid sé timchioll air.

he goes lazily about it, *b.* 265.

ro gab for baitsead Eireann.

he proceeded to baptize Ireland.

a. gebid for tecosc a daltai.

he begins (will begin) to instruct his fosterling.

o. ro gab maidm for U.

U. was defeated.

a. gabaid for glanrúni aduathmara do thabairt dó.

he proceeds to give (to swear to) him (by) the most awful mysteries.

rogab longes for Loch Eachach.

a fleet entered Loch Neagh.

gabad teas th' feirge gréim orra.

let the heat of thy displeasure take hold of them, *ps.* 69.

gréim do ġabáil air.

to lay hold of him, *b.* 398.

o. measaid sé nach féidir do dliġe ar bith gréim do ġabáil de.

he thinks no law can take hold of him, *b.* 398.

gaibthi ar gualainn.

caught by the shoulder.

an t-ainm do ġaḃ se air. — the name he assumed, *b.* **298.**

léinti Hollóind do ġabáil air. — to wear Holland shirts, *b.* **319.**

do ġaḃ sé air go rachad sé níos faide. — he pretended that he would go farther.

o. do léig seision air go rachad sé níos faide. — he " let on " that he would go farther, *l.* **24.**

o. ró-naoṁthacht do ġabáil ré hais. — to pretend to great holiness, *b.* **318.**

gabaim-se ar mo chorp agus ar m'anam thú ar ṁeaḃal do ḋeunaṁ ort aniu. — I take thee pledging my body and my life that no evil shall be done thee to-day, *dg.* **154.**

ατáid mórán do neithiḃ eile do ġabadar orra do choiṁeud. — many other things there be which they have received to hold, *mk.* **7.**

an ngeubthá ort féin a leithéide sin do ní do ḋeunaṁ? — would you offer to do such a thing? *b.* **511.**

an tan do ġábais ort an duine do ṡaorad. — when you undertook to save man, *Te Deum.*

gach uile ní do ġaḃ ḃur g-cairde chríost orra ar ḃur son. — everything your godfathers and godmothers undertook for you.

a n-gabáil na toisge sin orm. — in undertaking this business.

o. ġeabad-sa re m'ais soin do ḋeunad. — I'll undertake to do that.

o. atáim ar mo ṡáruġad, gaḃ do láiṁ mé. — I am oppressed, undertake for me, *Isaias,* **38.**

gabaim orm go m-bíonn cíos árd san tír. — I warrant that rent is high in this country.

o. do ḃríġ gur ġabusa rém 'ais forus feasa d'fʻaisnéis ar Éirinn. — because I have undertaken to narrate a history of Ireland, *K.'s preface.*

coronuccad Pedair do ġabáil do muintir Iae forro. — the religious family of Iona adopted S. Peter's tonsure, *fa.* **20.**

o. léig daṁ ar d-tús mo chead do ġabáil ag am' ṁuintir noch atá am' thiġ-se. — let me first go and bid them farewell who are at home at my house, *l.* **9.**

a. gaibid side céill for báas. — he thinks on death, is persuaded he is to die (?).

do gabad suas ar neaṁ arís é.

he was received up into heaven again, *mk.* 16.

neach do ġaḃáil ar neaṁaire.

to catch a person napping, *b.* 485.

do gaḃáil ar coimeirce.

to take under protection.

gabad an bás sealḃ orra.

let death take possession of them, *ps.* 55.

o. geuḃthar le fear oca agus fuigfiḋthear an fear eile.

the one shall be taken and the other left, *m.* 24.

ní maith gabáil ré pearsainn an drochduine.

it is not good to accept the person of the wicked, *pr.* 118.

gabaim-se ar mo chorp agus ar m'anam thú ar ṁeabal do deunaṁ ort aniu.

I take thee pledging my body and my soul that no evil shall be done thee to-day, *dg.* 154.

gabaim-se orm é ḃeith iomlán follán.

I warrant him to be safe and sound.

gabaim orm nach láṁfaid sé a deunaṁ.

I'll engage he will not dare to do it, *b.* 358.

do ġaḃail air féin, do ġaḃáil re hais.

to undertake, to enterprise, *b.* 192.

an n-geaḃtha ort féin a leith-éide sin do ní do deunaḋ?

would you offer to do such a thing? *b.* 511.

do ġaḃ seision ar n-eugcruais-ne air.

he took our infirmities, *m.* 8.

do ġaḃ Iosa colann n-daonna air.

Jesus assumed human nature.

a. gaibid armma Dé foiriḃ.

put ye on the armour of God.

gabaim a chorp ar choimir-cead mo ġaile agus mo ġaisge.

I take his body under the protection of my bravery and valour, *dg.* 152.

do ġaḃus cunntus sonnráḋach ar lochtaiḃ mo ḃeatha.

I took a particular account of the sins of my life.

a. gabaim nem ocus talam 'na fiadnaiḃ form.

I took heaven and earth as my witness.

ceangal aimsire do ġaḃáil ar árus.

to take a lease of a house, *b.* 401.

is iongnaḋ liom a laiġed ro ġaph ó Chenél Eogain tigernus for cách inossa.

I wonder how few of the C. E. have taken the lordship over all till now, *fa.* 18.

a. ma numgaibi ar charit. — if you take me for a friend.

a. do ġabáil taiġe fair. — to take a house from him, *fa.* 8.

di a gabáil ar Thuathaib Dé Danann. — to take it from the Tuatha De Danann.

an chrannócc do ġabáil la C. ar D. — the Cranog was taken by C. from D., 4 *Masters*, 1541.

ro gab láim ar a araid. — 'he commanded his charioteer,' *Ferdiad*, 422.

i lár na ciorcuille a n-gabthar léirṁeas uirre. — in the middle of the circle in which a clear view is got of her, *b.* 458.

longphort do ġabáil forra. — their camp was entered or taken, *fa.* 192.

trí chaogaid salm gach dia as ed gebeas ar Dhia. — three fifties of psalms every day is what he sings to God, *fa.* 84.

Verbs derived from **Gabhaim :—**

Tógbhaim, Fágbhaim, Faghbhaim, Dogheibhim, Congbhaim.

tógbaim an Tiġearna d' fiadnuise aír. — I take God to witness it, *Ephes.* 4.

tógbaid sé an iomad air féin. — he arrogates too much to himself, *b.* 37.

a. ro thóccaib a chíos riogda forru. — he levied his tribute on them.

o. sraith do leagad ar thír. — to tax a country, *b.*

fágbaim ort briathar agus buaid. — I leave thee victory and conquest, *ob.* 62.

d'fágbus ar a chur féin é. — I left it at his disposal, *b.* 167.

d'fágbus ar a thoil féin é. — I left it at his disposal, *b.* 167.

a b-fágbáil go hiomlán ar ucht an easboig. — to commit them entirely to the bishop.

d'fagbus garda ṁaith air. — I left a good guard on him, *b.* 248.

fágthar sé ar láiṁ na naṁad miltighe-sí. — he is left a prey to this dangerous foe, *d.* xix.

fágbaim thú ar do soláthar féin.

neach d'fágbáil ar deirid an rioth.

fágtha ar deirid; fágtha ar deire a b-fad ann rioth.

fágbaim a meas fút.

an té chongbas ar a beul atá sé críonna.

atáim ag congbáil orm féin.

a los an t-seanchusa do chongbáil ar bun.

ó pheacaidib uaibreacha congbaig ar ais do seirbíseach.

neach do chongbáil ar obair; rún do chongbáil ar ní.

o. gid bé ag a b-fuil dúil ann a beatha agus ré ar mían laethe maithe d'faicsin, congbad sé a theanga na tocht ó olc agus a beul ó meabail do labairt.

o. neach d'á chongbáil féin ó míochlu.

cia feudas é féin do chongbáil ó labairt?

ni fuaradar am ar biad amáin d'ithe.

am d'fagáil ar greamugad don chlachtad-sa.

d'fagáil a beatha ar allus a maillíde

ar chruth blais d'fagáil ar neithib neamda.

fagthar buaid ar A.

buaid imtheartha d'fagail air.

ar buaid fagáil orrainn.

fuarus clú mór do geall air.

I leave you to provide for yourself.

to leave a person behind in a race.

left behind; distanced in a race, *b.* 61, 251, 168.

I leave you to think, *b.*

he that refraineth his lips is wise.

I forbear, 1 *Thess.* 3, 2 *Cor.* 12.

in return for preserving the history, *k.* civ.

keep thy servant from presumptuous sins, *ps.* 19.

to keep one at work; to keep a thing to one's self, *b.* 381.

he that loves life, and would see good days, let him refrain his tongue from evil and his lips that they speak no guile, 1 *Peter*, 3.

to keep one's self unspotted, *b.* 381.

who can withhold himself from speaking? *Job.* 4.

they found no time so much as to eat food, *mk.* 6.

to find time to stick to that practice, *d.* 486.

to get his livelihood by the sweat of his brows.

on condition to find a relish in heavenly things.

A. is overcome.

to win a game against him, *b.* 431.

having overcome us, *ob.* 288.

I gained great reputation by it, *b.* 245.

ní fuair mé coir ar bith ar an duine so.

I have found no fault in this man, *l.* 23.

ní fuair mé cor ar bith air. ·

I find no twist in him.

ní fagaim-se cúis ar bith air.

I find no fault in him.

ní fagaim-se cúis ar bith ar an b-fear so.

I find no fault in this man, *l.* 23.

nó lá fá b-fuarabair eolus ar gras Dé go fírinneach.

since the day ye knew the grace of God in truth, *Colos.* 1.

d'a b-fuil grád na n-uile noch fuair eolus ar an fírinne.

who are loved by all that have found the truth, *2d. Ep. of St. John.*

múin dam gach ní atá riach-tanach chum eoluis d'fagáil ort.

teach me all that is necessary for knowing thee.

chum eoluis d'fagáil ar Dhia.

to know God, *d.* 462.

an méid d'eolus is éidir d'fag-áil ar Dhia, atá sé go follus ionnta-san.

that which may be known of God is manifest in him, *Rom.* 1.

o. abruid an muintir-se féin má fuaradar eugcóir ar bith ionnam.

let these same here say if they have found any evil doing in me, *A.* 24.

do fuair sé faill air,

he took an advantage of him, *ob.* 228.

an té bíos ollam do gnath ní féidir faill d'fagáil air go bráth.

he who is always ready can never be found wanting, or at fault.

is ionmuin leo fáilte d'fagáil ar na marguidib.

they love to get greetings in the markets, *m.* 22.

cóimeudaid sib ó na daonib lé n-ab ionmuin fáilti d'fagáil ar na margaidib.

beware of those who love to get salutations in the market-places, *mk.* 12.

tar éis fios d'faigáil dúinn ar theacht Iosa Chríost.

after we have known the coming of Jesus Christ.

no go b-fuigead A. fios air.

until A. should take cogni-sance of his case, *A.* 25.

gan t' fagáil acht flosgad beag ar ní.

to get but a glimpse of a thing, *b.* 262.

lo fuaramar an gaoth orra.

we got the wind of them, *b.* 254.

an tan do braith nach b-fuair
sé éinní a ngeall air.
creud fuarais mar ġeall air?
ní b-fuiġim-se aon ní a ngioll
air.
as é léiġeas fuair C. dóib ar
cheol na murdachann.

an uair fuair sé cách ar chaoi
meisġe.
fuair ós ceann chúig ceud
dearbráthair radarc air a n-
éinfeacht.
ionnas go b-fuiġead sgeula
oruib.
mar fuair an chnum radarc
air, tug sith sanntach air.

a b-faġad Ioseph ar a ṡaoir-
seacht acus muire ar a
gréis.
ní b-fuiġid sé sgeula ar a n-
dearnais go bráth.
ní cóir go b-fuiġead aon
ġnothuiġ tosach air.
fuaradar tosach orm.
do fuarus tuairim air.
do frith uain orm.

fuaradar iad d'uireasbà
orrtha.
is misde liom an meud ġeuba
sé air.
geabthar mise go maith ort.

do ġeibim amach eolus ar
neithib intleachtacha.
is caol an t-slíġe agus is beag
do ġeib eolus uirre.
do geib se locht ar gach duine.

when he found that he got
nothing by it, b. 253.
what did you get by it? b. 253.
I get nothing by it, b. 254.

this is the remedy which C.
got for them against the
music of the sirens, od.
when she found all in a state
of ebriety, dg. 54.
over five hundred brethren at
once saw him, 1 Cor. 15.

that I may hear of your
affairs, Philipp. 1.
when the worm got sight of
him it gave an eager spring
at him, dg. ii. 8.
what Joseph acquired by his
trade as a carpenter and
Mary by her needlework.
he shall never know what you
have done, dg. 60.
no business should take the
place of it, d. 476.
they got before me.
I had a hint of it. 1. 314.
I brought my hogs to a fine
market, b. 316.
they found that they were
missing, dg. 62.
I care not how much he will
get by it, b. 91, 327.
I shall deal well with you,
Gen. 32, cb. 273.
I find out knowledge of witty
inventions, pr. 8.
the way is narrow and few
there are that find it, m. 7.
he carps at every body,
b. 104.

do ġeíb se locht air.

o. ro ġab fotha aṁail faol fo chaorchaib.

ra ġabsat fa deoiġ for a' g-cloidṁib.

ro gabad cacht foraib.

é féin d'iomġabáil ar na ceithre ceannaib nathrach neiṁe úd.

do ġeabair luad go líonṁar ar an droing thuasl

he finds fault with him, k. xl.

he attacked them as a wolf (attacks) sheep,   fa. 166.

they took at last to their swords,   fa. 164.

they were put in bondage,
     An. Ulster, 864.

to guard himself against the four heads of that adder,
     s. 18

you sʰall find abundant meⁿ tion of the above persons,   k. 398.

Teidhim, I go.

d'eagla go reachad aca orra; d'eagla go rachad aca ort.

an uair do chonnaire se nach deachuid aige air.

dá n-deachad agad ar na Collaib.

an fá mo chuṁachtaib-se do dol ort?

M. do dol sluaġ doridise ar-chloinn Aeda; dol ar M.

o. d'éirġe suas air.

o. agus aṁail ná éirġead C. air.

do chuadar a n-easúṁla air.

ro cuas forra; ra cuas for Caer Ebroic.

do chuaid ainm oirdeirc air-sion.

Athair na soillse ar nach d-téid athruġad.

lest they should prevail over them; lest they should pre-vail over thee,   od.

when he saw that he prevailed not against him,   Gen. 32.

if you should prevail over the Collas.

is it because my power has prevailed over thee?

M. went again with a host against the sons of Aed; to go against M.,
     4 Mast., an. 1541, 1542.

to affront him,   b. 17.

as C. would not rise against him,   fa. 242.

they rebelled against him,
     Isaias, 63.

they were attacked; York was entered,   fa. 172, 192.

his name was spread abroad,
     mk. 6.

the Father of lights with whom is no variableness,
     James, 1.

nach deachaid bearna na muchad air le foirneart eachtrann.

that it was not interrupted or stifled by the violence of foreigners,   *k.* xcviii.

cisde ar nach racha caitheaṁ.

a treasure that faileth not,   *l.* 12.

a. docóith dígal forru; resíu docoith grád forru; *a.* oc mo théit-se for apstalacht.

punishment came on them; before they were ordained; at my going on the apostolic mission.

snáṁán admuid ag dul suas agus síos ar abainn.

a float of wood going up and down the river,   *b.* 222.

o ro choiméiriġ cách ar amus a chéile.

all rose up against each other,   *fa.* 172.

atá an t-olc so ag dul ar aġaid do síor is do ġnáth

this evil gains ground more and more,   *b.* 280.

atá sé ag dul ar aġaid; bíodmar ag dul ar aġaid go ceart go nuige sin; feudaid dul ar bur n-aġaid; ní deachaid sé aoin choiscéim ar aġaid; do rachad ar m'aġaid do réir mar chífead cúis.

he is progressing; we were getting on well till then; ye may go on; he did not go one step forward; I will proceed as I shall see cause,   *b.* 108.

ní rachfad ar m'aġaid.

I will not go further, *ob.* 398.

do dul ar aġaid a saidbrios; téid sé ar aġaid.

to increase in wealth; he succeeds,   *b.* 353, 286.

rachaid sé ar aġaid go díreach chum Comaoine.

he will go straight to communion.[1]

a n-deachaid aní sin ar aġaid dó?

did that thing succeed with him?

atáid na gadair ag dul ar aill.

the dogs are at a loss, *b.* 426.

neach do théid do'n taob ar aill.

one who goes from one side to the other,   *b.* 122.

is dúil dó dul ar aisdior; tá sé ag dul ar aisdior fada.

he is fond of travelling; he is going on a long voyage.

do bríġ nach b-fuil cara agam noch rachfainn ar a anacail iná ar a choimircead

since I have no friend under whose safeguard and protection I might go, *dġ.* 152.

do dol ar aoidecht amach.

to go to lodge out, *fa.* 22.

---

[1] In County Antrim a Catholic in asking whether he may go to Communion says, "Shall I gang forard?"

do chuadar na giollaide go teach ar aoideacht. | the servants went to a house to be entertained, *dg.* 126.

do chuadas-sa ar an áth. | he went to the ford, *dg.* 188.

do chuaid sé ar bárr an dúna. | he went to the top of the fort, *dg.* 60.

do dul a muda ar a bealach. | to lose his way, *b.* 426.

téidim ar beul. | I prevent, *ob.* 46a.

do dul ar bélaib a athar. | to oppose his father, 4 *Mast., p.* 1778.

do dul suas ar beurnuin. | to mount a breach, *b.* 475.

do chuadus ar bórd a luinge. | I went on board his ship, *b.* 77.

ní rachfaid críoch ar do bliadnaib. | thy years shall have no end, *Hebr.* 1.

do dul ar cáirde. | to run up a score, *b.* 180.

mar i n-deatach théid ar ceal do láthair. | but like smoke it passes away immediately, *s.* 198.

dul ar chinneamuin. | to draw lots, *b.* 427.

ra chuas uad ar cenn Múra. | Mura was sent for by him, *fa.* 14.

téidmíd ar ceal; rachaid an uile cholann ar cheal; acht mar deatach théid sé ar ceal go díreach; téid an faoisidin ar ceal ó'n marb amail neimní; d'á chur a g-céill go d-téid gach glóir saogalta ar ceal uainn i n-aimsir an euga. | we vanish, cease to live; all flesh shall perish; but as smoke it passes away at once; the confession (or praise) vanishes from the dead man as nothing to signify that every worldly glory passes away from us at the time of death, *s.* 66, 211, 198, 48.

do chuaid sé ar coigrig. | he went on a journey.

an té théid a n-urrugus ar choimthigeach. | he who goes security for a stranger, *pr.* 20.

is feárr duit dul asteach don beathaid ar leath-chois nó ar leathláim nó ar leathsúil. | it is better for thee to enter into life with one foot or one hand or one eye, *m.* 18, *mk.* 9.

do chuaid an Naom-óig ar cuairt fá n-a déigin. | the Blessed Virgin went to visit her, *d.* 384.

gan ar n-dul chugaib ar cuairt. | not to go on a visit to you, *Lir.* 35.

a. luid for cuairt.

ní théid an grád ar g-cúl choidche.

téidim ar g-cúl a n-áit dul ar agaid ; téidim ar g-cul a n-gnód a n-éiric dul ar agaid ; do dul ar g-cúl.

atá a sgéirh ag dul ar g-cúl.

do dul ar chúla aoin.

is gearr do théid ar dearmad.

do dul ar dilrhiann.

gíd b'é théid asteach ar an dorus.

do chuaid sé ar dorus na huarha do deunarh faire.

a. do imthecht foirib, O doir-sea !

dul tar a ais ar dúthchas a rhathar.

do chuaid sé ar earráid : feud-aid dul ar earráid.

bean do chuaid ar elod le D.

árhuil as go rachad sé ar fairrge.

do chuaid seision fá leith ar an b-fásach.

do chuaid sé fá leith ar fásach.

gan ar n-dul ar faoinneal ocus ar foluamain.

téideam ar foscad.

rachfuid asteach ar na fuin-eoga arhail gaduig.

do dul ar gárduin.

do dol for geltacht.

do dul asteach ar gníorh.

do dul asteach ar gníorhad.

---

he went on a visit.

charity never fails, 1 *Cor.* 13.

I go back instead of going forward ; I go back in a business instead of going forward ; to flinch,
b. 222, 265.

her beauty fades away, *b.* 205.

to go behind one, *b.* 265.

it is soon forgotten, *b.* 495.

to enter upon a design, *b.* 192.

he that entereth by the door,
j. 10.

he went to the door of the cave to keep watch, *dg.* 86.

to go through you, O doors !

to go back to his mother's country, *dg.* 120.

he hath erred ; they may err.

a woman who eloped with D ,
k. xxviii.

as if he were going to the sea,
A. 17.

he withdrew into the wilder-ness, *l.* 5.

he went aside into a desert place, *l.* 9.

without our going mad and distracted.

let us get under shelter.

they shall enter in at the windows like a thief, *Joel,* 2

to mount guard, *b.* 248.

to run mad, *fa.* 40.

to enter upon an action,
b. 192.

to enter upon an action,
b. 192, 194

téid sé ar imthelgud.
ní theidim suas ar mo leabaid.

I climb not up into my bed, *ps.* 13².

a. docóid O. dochum Póil for longis ; *o*, luid for longais.
do dul ar lorg guasachta nuad.

O. went to Paul into exile ; he went into exile.
to go in quest of new adventures, *b.* 562.

dul ar marcuiġeacht ar each ; stíorróip. i. gleus re dul ar marcuiġeacht go heusga,
o. do marcuiġeacht ar múillid.

to ride a horse; stirrup, that is, a means of riding easily, *b.* 624.
to ride upon a mule.

ag dul ar mearuġad.
rachaid furachus an drochduine ar meath.

going astray, mistaking, *b.* 466.
the expectation of the wicked shall perish, *pr.* 10.

a. dothei for menmain

that shall come into his mind.

do luid ar a mhuineul agus do phóg é.

he fell on his neck and kissed him, *Gen.* 33.

do chuala mé teacht ort lé héisteacht na cluaise.

I have heard of thee by the hearing of the ear, *Job* 42.

ní tiucfáidthear thar chroibel nó thar pheurlaib.

no mention shall be made of coral or pearls, *Job* 28.

is form féin doróg hi tossuch.

it is of myself I shall speak first, *Wb.* 7.

go n-deachaid sé suas ar neamh ; do chuaid síos go hifrion, do chuaid suas ar neamh ; ní rachaid na buirb ar neamh.

that He ascended into heaven, He descended into hell, He ascended into heaven ; the proud shall not go to heaven.

o. rachaid na tonna suas go nuige neamh, agus síos arís gus an aigeun.

the waves shall go up to heaven and down again to the deep.

o. an lucht theíd síos chum na fairrge.

that go down to the sea.

do dul ar neartlámh leis an námhuid.

to grapple with the enemy, *b.* 173.

dobeir sé tuairim maith damh re dul ar mo dara réim.

he gives me a good hint to proceed to my second point, *b.* 314.

ní théid dligead ar an riachtanus.

necessity has no law, *b.* 488.

dul ar seachnaḋ.
do ḋul ar seachain ó ṁaith do
deunaṁ.
na hapstalachta ó a n-deachaiḋ
I. ar seachrán.
ní deachus ar seachrán ó'd
aitheantaiḃ-si.
ó a n-deachaiḋ I. ar seachrán
do chuaḋmar ar seachrán ó do
ṡlígthiḃ mar chaorchaiḃ.
an ṁéid do chuaiḋ ar seachrán
do threoruġaḋ go slíge na
fírinne.
o. do báḋar ar seachrán.
do ḋul ar siuḃal.
a né nach rachaiḋ sé ar na
sléiḃthiḃ d'iarraiḋ an cao-
rach.
do chuaiḋ sé suas 'na aonur ar
ṡliaḃ do ḋeunaṁ urnaiġde.
neach do dul amúġa ar a ṡlíge.
do ḋul amach ar thaisdioll.

do ḋul ar theachtaireacht.
a. luid-sium for teched.
cá huair rachas tú ar an tír.

rachaḋ mé ar an tír.
do ḋul ar a thóin.
a. ní for torbe n-imdibe dotéit-
som,
dul ar uaṁannaiḃ iomdaiḃ.

do chuaiḋ sé ar uiṁir na marḃ.

to escape,   b. 203.
to play the truant,   b. 541.
of the Apostleship from which
  J. strayed away,   A. 1.
I have not swerved from thy
  commandments,   ps. 119.
since J. went astray,   A. 1.
we have strayed from thy
  ways like sheep.
to bring into the way of truth
  all that have erred.

they were astray.
to go away,   b. 225.
will he not go into the mountains to seek the sheep,
                              mk. 18.
he went alone up into a
  mountain to pray,   m. 14.
to mistake one's way,   b. 466.
to set out on a journey,
                              b. 231.
to go with a message,   b. 194.
he took to flight.
when will you go to the country? (German auf das
  Land).
I will go to the country.
to flinch,   b. 222.
it is not of the advantages of
  circumcision he speaks.
to enter or attack many crypts,
                              fa. 152.
he is gone over to "the ma-
  jority,"   b. 268.

Tigim, I come.[1]

do theacht orruinn (gan fíos).	to surprise us.
do theacht asteach air.	to incroach upon him, *b.* 353.
a. nach d-tiocfaḋ forru tria bithu.	that he would not come against them ever.
ní thiocfa duine ar bith ortsa do ḋeunaṁ uilc ḋuit.	no man shall set on thee to hurt thee, *A,* 18.
táinic Coirpre timchioll na bruinde ortsa.	C. came against you round the court, *dg.* 186
ní tainig críde neich diḃ fair.	the heart of any of them did not move towards him, *fa.* 35.
tiocfaḋ a chroiḋe orra.	his heart would move (with tenderness) towards them, *s.* 134.
cad é an aicíd tháinic air? nó	what was his disease?
go d-tigiḋ an bás gan fíos orra.	until death surprises them.
giḋ bé ní do ḋeuna sé tiocfaiḋ biseach air.	whatsoever he doeth it shall prosper, *ps.* 1.
brionnglóid do thig air ann a chodla.	a vision which comes to him in his sleep, *b.* 505.
tháinic bród mór air.	he was much elated.
an tan thiucfas cathuġad air.	when he shall be tempted, *b.* 416.
tá eagla orm go d-tiocfa cith orrainn.	I fear we shall get a shower.
ná tigeaḋ cos an uabair orm ;	let not the foot of pride come against me, *ps.* 37.
atá eagla agus criothnuġaḋ ar d-teacht orm.	fear and trembling are come upon me, *ps.* 55.
tig critheagla do ġnáth um' chroiḋe,	my heart always begins to ache, *b.* 303.
táinic a chruth féin air.	his own form came on him, *dg.* 148.
ní thiocfa díoġḃáil ort.	you shall come to no harm, *b.* 495.

---

[1] This common word is not in De Vere Coney's Dictionary!

mar do gráduiġ sé easgaine, tigead sí air.

as he loved cursing, let it happen to him, *ps.* 109.

re techt gráid forru.

before their ordination.

canas tánic duibse fis fair sin.

how did ye come to know that?

Tochm. Moméra, 152.

biaid sé go lór chum teachta suas air.

this will be enough to live on. *b.* 192.

tháinic meubán orm.

I got dizzy, *b.* 169.

táinig mian na n-áirnead ar Shadb.

Sadb longed for the sloes, *dg.* 124.

táinic tinneas orra féin.

they fell ill.

ní thig uath uirre go bráth.

it is never eclipsed, *b.* 483.

do theacht ar aġaid ; leanb bías ag teacht ar aġaid ; tá sé ag dul ar g-cúl a n-áit teacht ar aġaid ; atá armáil na namad ag corruiġe ar a n-aġaid.

to grow ; a forward child ; he is going backward instead of going forward ; the enemy's army moves forward, *b.* 280, 232.

tig ar ais ; cá huair thiucfas sí ar a hais?

come back ; when will she come back?

tainic ar amus Adamnáin.

She came to Adamman, *fa.* 102.

a Chríst mac Dé, tiagamuit uile ar h-amus.

O Christ, Son of God, we all fly to thy protection, *ob.* 22.

tánac-sa for a amus.

I came to him.

ní tháinig sé ar ammus an longphuirt.

he did not come towards the camp, *fa.* 122.

ag teacht leis ar an m-bréig sin.

agreeing with him in that lie, *k.* 26.

focail do thig ar aoin chéill.

synonyms—words which agree in meaning, *b.* 631.

tigid an triur-sa ré chéile ar aon ní.

these three agree in one, 1 *John,* **5.**

tiagair ar a cenn uainde

let us send for them.

táinic ar a g-cionn ar an t-sliġid.

he came to meet them on the the way, *fa.* 72.

tiagam bar ar claidbib tromma.

let us resort to our heavy swords, *Ferdiad,* 444.

tiagam ar comairce Shéasair ;
a n-deachaid tú ar comairce
Shéasair ? is d'ionnsaiġe
Shéasair rachas tú.

I appeal to Cæsar ; hast thou
appealed to Cæsar ? unto
Cæsar shalt thou go, *A.* 25.

tig fós úġdar oile ré seanchus
ar an g-cómáirioṁ g-ceudna.

another historical writer agrees
with the same computation,
k.

gach caor dá d-tig ar an g-
crann biḋ buaḋa iomḋa aco.

all the berries that grow on the
tree have many virtues, *dg.*

tainic tionól mór ar crechaib ;
tangattar na Déisi ar
crechaib 'san b-ferann sin.

a great muster came to commit depredations ; the Deisi
came to plunder in that
land, *fa.* 168, 236.

tánic longes for cuan Lumnig.

a fleet came into the harbour
of Limerick.

an uair thuiteas na rógairi
amach tiocfaiḋ duine
macánta ar a chuid féin ;
má thig sé ar éisdeacht go
brath.

when rogues fall out an honest
man will get his own ; if it
ever comes to the pinch,
b. 538.

ernáil táinic ar pháis Chriost.

the sign which marked out
the passion of Christ,
ob. 223.

ga gasced ar a ragam indiu ?
ga gasced for a ragam indiu?
ga gasced ir-ragam i festa ?

what is the kind of arms to
which we shall resort to-day?
what is the kind of arms to
which we shall resort now ?
Ferdiad. 444.

neach do theacht suas ar a
ġusdal.

to live on one's income, *b.* 418.

teccait for irair Deimne.

they come to look for Deimne.

creud é an toisg fá a d-tánga-
dar ar an láthair sin.

what is the business for which
they came to that place ?
dg. 200.

tá sé ag teacht ar láthair.

it is forthcoming, *b.* 231.

tigid-si ar leith go hionad
uaigneach.

come ye apart to a desert
place, *mk.* 231.

do theacht suas ar luibeannaib
agus ar freuṁaib.

to live upon roots and herbs,
b. 418.

tiaġaid na Danair for longphort na Lochlann.

the Danes enter the camp of
the Lochlanns, *fa.* 122.

tig an t-seanaois ar mailltriall; tig se ar marcuiġeacht ar reithe dub cúl ar aġaid.
a. má beid ní di rúnaib dothéi ar menmain ind fir.

old age creeps on; he comes riding backwards on a black ram, *b* 142, 236.
if something of the mysteries should come into the mind of the man.

tigid na huilc ar muin a chéile; tig buairead ar muin buairid.

troubles come on the back of each other; trouble comes on the neck of trouble.

a. teacht for nem; tiagait for neiphní.

to go to heaven; they come to nought or vanish.

neach do theacht suas ar a obair; do theacht suas ar phreumaib.

to live by one's work; to live upon roots, *b.* 418.

tháinic an solus ar an saoġal; is é so an fáith do bí chum teachta ar an t-saoġal.

the light came into the world; he was the prophet that should come into the world.

tiaġait ar seachrán.

they go astray, *ps.* 58.

tiaġaid for sescenn ba nessa.

they go to a neighbouring morass, *fa.* 146.

do tháinic na ceudfada ar an m-baile do sgrios.

the votes went for the destruction of the city, *b.* 652.

tig sé suas ar a śaothar.

he lives upon his labour, *b.* 388.

isé an cheud tosach Rómánach do tháinic ar thalam na m-Bretan.

he is the first Roman general that came into the land of the Britons.

do theacht suas ar thoraid.

to live upon fruit, *b.* 238.

is form féin doreg hi tossuch.

it is of myself I shall speak first, *Wb.* 7*d.*

an tan do chualaid sí teacht ar Iosa.

when she had heard Jesus spoken of, *mk.* 5.

do thionnsgainn Iosa teacht thar Eoin ris an g-cóimthionól.

Jesus began to speak to the multitude concerning John.

o. cionnas chreidfid siad annsan té nach g-cualadar teacht thairis?

how shall they believe in him of whom they have not heard? *Rom.* 10.

ag teacht ar na neithib-si.

speaking of these things.

do b'féidir gurb air so atá an chaint sin Iob ag teacht.

perhaps this passage of Job's looks this way, *b.* 424.

ag teacht ar abainn nó ar thobar ; ag teacht ar thinneas. — in speaking of a river or a well; speaking of sickness, *b.* 405, 415.

gan teacht oruibsi. — not to speak of you, 2 *Cor.* 9.

creud iad na cómráidte-sí ar a b-fuilti ag teacht eadruib féin. — what are these discourses that you hold one with another?

creud iad na comairle-si ar a b-fuilti ag teacht eadruib fëin? — what are these communings which ye have among you? *l.* 24.

o. ciod an seanachas so a th' agaib ri chéile? (*Scotch*) — what are these discourses that you hold one with another?

ag teacht ar na neithib do bean ré ríogacht Dé. — speaking of the things pertaining to the kingdom of God, *A.* 1.

do chuala mé teacht ortsa go d-tuigeann tú aisling chum a eidirmínige. — I have heard say of thee that thou understandest a dream to interpret it, *Gen.* 41.

tiocfam ann so go haithgearr ar an tres persain. — we will speak here briefly of the second person, *Parrthas an Anma,* 95.

ní thiucfidear orm. — no mention will be made of me, *ob.* 477.

rob uabar tuidecht 'na chrích ar Cerball. — it was pride, to come into his territory against Cearball, *fa.* 220.

croíde Dé do thuideacht orra. — God's heart to turn towards them, *s.* 125.

do thocht ar an Sráth m-bán. — to go to Strabane, 4 *Mast. an.* 1606.

ná héirig asteach ar fearann na n-dílleacht. — enter not into the field of the fatherless, *pr.* 23.

o. éirig suas ar an sliab árd. — get up into the high mountain, *Isaias,* 40.

Imthigim, I go, I go away.

ní feas dúinn creud do imthig air. — we know not what is become of him, *ex.* 32.

d'imtheacht ar daonib eile ; d'ar imthig orra. — to have happened to other people ; which happened to them, *L.* 56, 62.

cad é d'imthiġ ar do chuid peanna? — what has become of your pen?

d'imthiġ sé ar aḋbar dó féin. — he is gone to seek his fortune.

imthiġid ar a n-aġaiḋ; imthiġ go díreach ar aġaiḋ. — they pass on; go straight on.

imthíġeas ar an ainm sin. — I went by that name, *b.* 97.

imthiġ ar hais. — go back.

d'imthiġ sé ar aisdior nó ar turus. — he is gone on a journey, *b.* 268.

d'imthiġ a fearg ar ceal. — his anger is over, *b.* 518.

d'imtheacht ar cheithre gníd. — to go upon all fours, *b.* 234.

d'imthiġeadar rompa ar a g-cúl. — they went away backwards, *Isaiah,* 1.

o. do ṡiúbal ar deiriḋ. — to march in the rear, *b.* 445.

ro imiġ ar eachdra. — he went on an expedition, *ob.* 4.

imthiġid ar feaḋ an doṁain uile. — go ye into the whole world.

d'imtheacht ar ṁallṁuir. — to go adrift, *b.* 175.

mar do imthiġeadar na haingil ar neaṁ. — as the angels were gone away into heaven, *l.* 2.

o. d'imthiġ sé chum siúbail; d'imtheacht ar siúbal; d'imthiġ sé ar siúbal agus deargnait ann a chluais. — he went away; to get away; he went away with a flea in his ear, *b.* 500, 254, 221.

d'imthiġ sé arís ar an t-sliab 'na aonur. — He went again into the mountain himself alone.

teagaisg leanb a d-taob na slíġe air ar cóir dá imtheacht. — train up a child in the way he should go, *pr.* 22.

d'imtheacht ar smeurracht roiṁe. — to go groping along, *b.* 279.

ar n-imtheacht daoib ar na sráidib. — ye going out into the streets, *l.* 10.

neach imthiġeas ar a thoil féin. — a libertine, one who does as he likes, *b.* 408.

d'imthiġ sé ar turus. — he went on a journey, *b.* 268.

ar eagla go n-imtheochad tubuiste air. — lest mischief might befall him, *Gen.* 42,

o. má beanan tubuiste do. — if mischief befall him, *Gen.* 42.

imthiġeam don Bhetléem. — let us go to Bethlehem, *l.* 2.

Fillim.[1] Iompoigim. Casaim.
Teagmhnim, Tárla.

fillid ar bur g-croide (30); ná fill ar an láim deis nó chlé. athruig do chos ó'n olc; *a.* fillead for a láim n-deis; fillid sé ar laethib a ógántachta

do fill sé chum an phuill; do fill sé ar a dearbráithrib; do fill sé uirre ar an t-slíge; do fill orra arís; do fill ar a chliamuin; léig damsa fillead ar mo dearbraithrib; do fill go crích Egipte; fill don Egipt.

d'fillead ar phréim mo chomrad; d'fill sé an treas uair ar an tobar; fillid sé orra féin a g-cionnta; d'fillinn mo lám ar a n-eascáirdib; fillead beag na lám ar a chéile chum codalta.

na seólta d'fillead ar a chéile.

cia aca do na naoim chum a b-fille tú?

o. do fan Muire na fochair timchioll thrí mios agus d'fill sí d'a tig féin; fillid sé mórán do chlannaib Israel chum an Tigearna a n-Dia féin.

return ye to your heart; turn not to the right or left, remove thy foot from evil; to turn to his right hand; he shall return to the days of his youth.

he returned unto the pit; he returned unto his brethren; he turned unto her by the way; he returned to them again; he returned to his father-in-law; let me return to my brethren; he returned to the land of Egypt; return into Egypt.

to return to my subject; he returned the third time to the well; he shall recompense them their wickedness; I would have turned my hand against their enemies; a little folding of the hands to sleep.

to furl the sails.

to whom of the saints wilt thou turn?

Mary abode with her about three months, and returned to her own house; many of the children of Israel shall he turn to the Lord their God.

---

[1] To diminish the bulk and price of this book, I henceforth omit references and give only a few typical examples, marking in parenthesis the number which I have collected, when they are many.

do fill Ioseph don Egipt ; do
filleadar a slíġe eile d'a d-
tír féin ; tárla ar an t-slíġe
'san tíġ ósta gur chas an
Tiġearna air.

ar g-casaḋ orra d'Iosa do im-
ḋearg sé iad ; casaiḋ péisteog
ar fear a saltairt ; do chas sé
air ; casaḋ orm iad ; sé so an
fear do chas orrainn a n-dé.

o. casaḋ liom é ; ar casaḋ leat
í ? casfaithear linn iad ; o.
nior casaḋ ḋaṁ a n-áit ar
biṫ daoine buḋ carthanaiġe.

mar iompaiġeas madraḋ ar a
sceaṫraiġ, mar sin iompoi-
ġeas an t-amadán ar a leiṁe ;
má iompóiġmíd air féin le
croiḋe iomlán ; iompuiġ do
ṡúile trócaireacha orruinne ;
ar n-iompóḋ leice móiṙe dó
ar ḋorus an tuama ; do
iompuiġ sé leac ar ḋorus an
túama.

do bí fearg ort, iompóiḋ thú
féin chugainn arís ; gach
uile ḋuine iompóchas chuige
ré aithriġe ó chroíḋe.

ionntaiġ ar an láiṁ chlí.

croíḋe aoin d'ionntóġaḋ ar
Dhia ; gíd bé taob ar a n-
ionntócham sin féin.

do ionluit sé leac ar ḋorus an
tuama.

do chuaid an chathair uile
amach do theaġṁáil ar Iosa.
do chuaid suas do theaġ-
ṁáil ar Israel, a aṫair ; do
chuaid amach do theaġṁáil
ar an b-fear nuaphósda.

Joseph returned into Egypt ;
they returned another way
to their own land ; it came
to pass by the way in the
inn that the Lord met him.

and Jesus turned to them and
rebuked them ; a worm turns
on the man who treads on
it ; he met him ; I met them ;
this is the man we met
yesterday.

I met him ; did you meet her
we shall meet them ; I never
met anywhere more friendly
people.

as a dog returns to his vomit,
so a fool returneth to his
folly ; if with a perfect heart
we turn unto Him ; turn thy
merciful eyes towards us ;
having rolled a great stone
to the door of the sepulchre ;
he rolled a stone to the
door of the sepulchre.

thou hast been displeased ;
turn thee again unto us ;
all that with hearty repentance turn unto Him.

turn to the left hand.

to turn one's heart to God ;
which way soever we turn
ourselves.

he rolled a stone unto the door
of the sepulchre.

the whole city went out to meet
Jesus (25) ; he went up to
meet Israel, his father ; they
went forth to meet the bride-
groom.

tárla a n-dán di teagṁail ar an g-cuid don ṁachaire noch fa le Bóas ; dá d-teagṁaim air ; an cheud baile theagṁas ort (nó duit).

her hap was to light on a part of the field belonging unto Boas; if I should meet him ; the first town you meet.

do theagṁuid sé orm lé cinneaṁuin ; má theagṁann dias agaib ar aon focal ar talaṁ a d-timcheall gach uile ní iarruid siad

I met him by chance ; if two of you agree on earth as touching anything that they ask.

áit a d-teagṁuid dá śruith ar a chéile.

a place where two streams meet.

tháinic mé amach do theag- ṁáil riotsa agus fuair mé thú ; má theagṁann riot daṁ.

I came forth to meet you and I have found you (15) ; if you meet an ox.

teagṁad mathġaṁuin ar g-caill a cuileán ré duine níos luaithe ná amadán ionn a leiṁe ; teigéoṁad-sa leis ar thalaṁ ar bioth a Saxaib.

let a bear robbed of her whelps meet a man, rather than a fool in his folly ; I will meet him on any ground in England.

is lúthġáireach liom teagṁáil leat; téid sé ar a aġaid do theagṁáil ris na fearaib armtha; an cheud uair arís theagóṁaoid re a chéile.

I am glad to meet you ; he goeth on to meet the armed men ; the next time we shall meet together.

cia theagóṁad daṁ acht a leithéid-se do duine? do deachtaiġ sé teagṁáil daṁ a n-diu ; teagṁad daṁsa do réir do bréithre-si ; ní theagṁaid sin d'aoinneach acht d'amadánaib.

whom should I meet but such a one? (15); he appointed to meet me to-day ; be it done unto me according to thy word; that befalls none but fools.

ní féidir tiobuisde is mó do theagṁáil d'a g-clainn ; teigcóṁuid míśeun duit ; cionnas beannuiġeas tú don choṁarsain ag teagṁáil di.

no greater evil can befall their children ; misfortune will happen to you; how do you salute your neighbour when meeting him,

deunaid faire do chum nach d-teigceaṁad a g-cathuġad sib.

watch lest ye enter into temptation.

tárla go d-tárla sluaġ mór air-
sion ; tárla óglach as an g-
cathraiġ air.

tárladar deichneabar lóbar air
do šeas a b-fad uad ; nach
ar thárlaid sgeula deorada
ort ar teacht a d-tir duit ;
ao. óen ní forsa tárla
m'aire-sea and ; tárla lorg
muice alta ar ġadar.

do thárladar ar meisge go tarcuisneach ; tárla daille ar
chuid d'Isráel.

a. do rala sé for aes cerdai ; do
rála menma a mathar fair ;
cid dorála ar bar n-aire.

thárlaiġ mé don duine uasal
agus d'á ṁnaoi ; thárla
neach do diongṁála duitsi ;
thárlaid cinneaṁain ró-
uathbásach daṁ.

thárla fáilte róṁíochair dó ;
do thárlaid fiabrus creathach
dó ; creud thárlaid dot'
dearbrathair ?

o. do bain anachain dó.

thárla tròcaire agus fírinne ré
chéile ; tárla sé rinn ; do
thárlid diúltad ris ; do rala
a chos fria cloich.

it came to pass that much
people met him (25) ; a
man out of the city met him.
ten lepers met him who stood
afar off ; have you not met
with strange news on land-
ing ; one thing which at-
tracted my attention ; a
dog came across the track
of a wild hog.
they happened to be basely
drunk ; blindness has
happened to part of Israel.
he meets artificers ; the mother's
mind was fixed on him ;
what is it that has attracted
your attention ?
I met the gentleman and his
lady (10) ; you have met
your match ; a very strange
accident befel me.

he met with a very fine re-
ception ; he was attacked
with ague; what has become
of your brother ?
an accident befel him.
mercy and truth have met
together ; he met with us ;
he met with a refusal ; his
foot struck against a stone.

Eigim, Glaodaim, Goirim, Gairmim, Gairim, and its Compounds (Freagraim, Fuagraim, Arfócraim, Forcongraim, Tagraim).

Freagraim and fógraim are generally followed by *do* or the accusative.

as na haigeunaib d'éiġ mé ortsa (12); is cosṁuil é ré garlachaib śuideas ar na marguidib agus éiṁġeas ar a g-compánachaib; do éiġ M. ar an Tiġearna fá na loisgionnaib; do éiġṁeadar na daoine ar Fháraoh d' iarraid aráin; atâ guth fola do dearbrathar ag éiġṁe ormsa as an d-talaṁ.

out of the deep I have called unto thee; it is like unto children sitting in the markets and crying unto their fellows; M. cried unto the Lord because of the frogs; the people cried to Pharaoh for bread; the voice of thy brother's blood crieth unto me from the ground.

éiġim chugadsa, deun deithfir chugam an tan ġairim ort.

I call upon thee, haste thee unto me when I cry unto thee (4).

do choṁairc mé chugad agus do léiġis tú mé; cluin guth m'athchuinge an uair chóṁaircfead chugad; ag cóṁairc chum na sliab.

I cried unto thee and thou hast healed me; hear the voice of my petition when I shall cry unto thee; crying to the mountains.

na peacaide sgreadas ar Dhia ag iarraid díoġaltais; do sgreadadar ormsa; do sgreadadar ar Fháro.

the sins that cry to God for vengeance; they cried out unto me; they cried out to Pharaoh.

an uair sgréuchuid a eoin óga ar Dhia.

when his young birds cry unto God.

glaod air chugam; glaodaid sibse Tiġearna ormsa; is ortsa do ġlaodmaíd, is chugadsa chuirimíd suas ar n-osnaidthe; Thadġ Gaodlach is mó ġlaodaid na daoine orm; do ġlaoid mé air.

call him to me; ye call me Lord; to thee do we cry, to thee do we send up our sighs (15); Tadhg Gaodhlach is what people mostly call me; I gave him a call.

do ġlaoid tú drochainme orm.

you called me bad names.

do ġlaoiḋ sé ar an m-bás a theacht ; do ḃí mise Eoin 'san oileán ar a n-glaoidtear Patmos ; tá an chroch ag glaoḋaḋ air ; glaoḋaḋ ar deaṁnaiḃ suas.

cluinfid an Tiġearna an tan ġoirfead air (18) ; agus tárla gur ġoir sí ar ṁuintir an tiġe ; is ar ainm an Tiġearna goirfead mé ; guiḋfead mo Dhia agus goirfead air ; goirfead ar an Tiġearna noch is fiú a ṁolaḋ ; ní fuláir gur ab é Dia do ġoirfeas air.

an tan éitiġeas an ġairm chum ar ġoir Dia air ; do ġoir sé orruinn agus ġaḃ linn mar chloinn dó féin ; do ġoir sí ar ṁuintir a tige, agus do labair sé riú ; do ġoir sé orm chum na staide-se an t-slán- uiġthe ; an tan do ġoir orr- tha chum aithríġe ; do ġoir Pharoh ar Mhaoise ; maiseaḋ cionnas aithneochas neach go n-goireann Dia air?

thug ainm air ag goirm air " Mara."

goirthi-si Tiġearna díomsa ; is beannuiġthe lucht na sí- othcháns do ḋeunaṁ óir goirfithear clann Dé díob ; goirfid na huile ġíne bean- nuiġthe díom ; creud fá n- goireann tú maith díomsa ; do ġoir mé cáirde díob, ní ġoirfe mé seirḃísiġe díob ;

he called on death to come ; I John, was in the isle which is called Patmos ; the gallows groans for him ; evocation of spirits.

the Lord will hear me when I shall invoke him ; and it came to pass that she called unto the men of the house ; I will invoke the name of the Lord ; I will pray to my God and call on him ; I will call on the Lord who is worthy to be praised ; it is necessary that God should call him.

when he refuses to embrace the calling to which God calls him ; he hath called us and adopted us as his children ; she called unto the people of the house and spoke to them ; he hath called me to this state of salvation ; when he calls them to repentance ; Phar- aoh called Moses ; how then can one know that God calls him ?

he gave it a name, calling it " Mara."

ye call me Lord ; blessed are the peacemakers for they shall be called the children of God ; all generations shall call me blessed ; why do you call me good ? I have called you friends, I will not call you servants.

G

creud fá n-goirthear ceinn-pheacaide díob.

why are they called capital sins ?

ionnas gur ab a n-Antíochia do goiread ar tús Críostuigthe do na deisciopluib.

so that it was in Antioch the disciples were first called Christians.

cia d'á n goireann tú peacad mainneachtnaig ; o. do guireas chugadsa ; chuige-sean do goireas rém' beul.

what do you call a sin of omission ; unto Thee I have cried ; I called unto him with my mouth.

goir an lucht oibre agus tabair dóib a d-tuarasdal ; do goir sé an fear chuige ; do goir sí máthair an leinb.

call the labourers and give them their hire ; he called the man to himself ; she called the child's mother.

do gáir me chugadsa; chugadsa gáirfeas mé a Thigearna mo charraig ; gairfid siad ormsa acht ní freigeora mé.

I have cried unto Thee ; unto thee will I cry, O Lord, my rock ; they shall call upon me, but I will not answer.

gairim ort.

I call on thee, I cry to thee.

gairmim orruib a leith Chríost (20) ; gairmfead air ar n-imtheacht dam ; is cóir dib gairm air chum seanmóracha d'éisteacht ; oruibsi a daoine atáim ag gairm agus chum mac an duine atá mo guth ; ar n-gairm orrainn dod' focal naomtha-sa.

I call you in Christ's behalf ; I will call on him as I go along ; ye shall call upon him to hear sermons ; unto you, O men, I call, and my voice is to the sons of men ; we being called by thy holy word.

ar b-fágail a feasa sin don t-sagart, caithfid gairm air agus sgeul do thabairt dó gan lámad ar aon chor theacht ; is cóir do gairm orra chum an uile díthcheall do deunam lé beith folum-tha a m-bréithir Dé ; cibé am ar mian lé Dia gairm air ; atá sé ag gairm orrainn chum leasuigthe.

the priest having knowledge thereof, shall call him and advertise him not in any wise to come ; he is to call upon them to use all diligence to be instructed in the word of God ; whensoever it shall please God to call him ; he calleth us to amendment.

cíd bé ar bioth is gairm dó.

howsoever he be styled.

gairmiḋ sé cloḋaire díom ; a
ainm dílios do ġairm do gac
ní ; ní fiú mise feasda do
ṁac-sa do ġairm díom ; leas-
ainm do ġairm dó.

ɔ. do ġaireadar chum an Tiġearna ionn a n-anacair ; do
ġairmeas é chum a focail do
deunaṁ go maith ; is mian
leis an riġ a choṁḋáil do
ġairm.

ag freagra ar Fhilip a duḃairt
sé ; mo freagra ar Strabo
gurab breug dó a ráḋ ; go
b-feasar a b-freagra orm ;
mar freagraḋ air sin ; ní
tardsat freagra fuirri.

an freagra do ḃeirim ar gac
sgél ; do freagair Píolait
dóiḃ ; aṁuil freagreas aġaiḋ
d'aġaiḋ oile annsan uisge,
mar sin freagraiḋ croiḋe
ḋuine do chroiḋe oile ;
freigeoraiḋ mé focal d'fir
mo choiriġthe ; do freagair
Josa é ; freagair mé.

d'fuagair sé ar sluaġaiḃ
Eirionn ; ar a fócair anuas.

ra fuagair cách ar a chéle ;
d'fógra briste oruiḃse ; ro
fuagratar cath for Saxoin ;
cuirid F. teachta d'fuagraḋ
catha ar D. ; fuacraiḋ
comrac oenfir foir.

coinniollḃathaḋ d'fuagra air.

ro fuacraḋ sluaiġeḋ direacra
uaḋ for Leith Cuinn ;

he calls me a rogue ; to call
everything by its proper
name ; I am no more
worthy to be called thy son ;
to call him a nickname.

they cried unto the Lord in
their trouble ; I called on
him to make good his word ;
the king intends to call his
Parliament.

answering Philip, he said ;
my answer to Strabo is that
it is a lie for him to say it ;
until I shall know their
answer to me ; in answer to
that ; they did not give her
an answer.

the answer I give to every
tale ; Pilate answered them ;
as in water face answereth
face, so the heart of man
answereth another man ;
I shall make answer to
my blasphemers ; Jesus
answered him ; hear me.

he cried to the hosts of
Erin ; of which he admon-
ishes above.

they challenged each other ;
to cry alarm against you ;
they challenged the Saxons
to battle ; F. sends messengers to proclaim battle
against D. ; he challenges
him.

to pronounce excommunica-
tion against him.

an irresistible hosting was proclaimed by him to Conn's

fóigeorad as mo theaġ é.

Half, *i.e.*, he ordered L. C. to muster; I shall forbid him my house.

is for óis tuaithe arfócarar.

is the laity that are admonished.

d'erfuaccra na hesérgi for in cined n-doenda; forcongraim fort érgi; forcongra fair gan O'Neill do ġairm de; ro forcongair forru.

to proclaim the resurrection to the human race; I order thee to rise; he enjoins him not to be called O'Neill; he commanded them.

inté forsa forcongair; intí forsa forcongarar; ag tagra ar imirt; cia thusa thagras a n-aġaid Dé? nár agrar orra é!

the person whom he orders; he who is commanded; speaking of play; who art thou that disputest with God? may it not be laid to their charge!

Labraim, Adeirim, Ráidim, Aithrisim, Innisim, Foillsiġim, Canaim, Tráchtaim, Sgríobaim, Cuimniġim, Smuainim.

labraid ar a iongantaiḃ uile (44); as ar Chríost agus an eaglais labraim-se; ní labraim orruiḃ uile; labraim go maith air ós a chómair féin.

talk of all his wonders; it is concerning Christ and the Church I speak; I do not speak of you all; I speak well of him before his face.

túinġearrthóir, neach do labras go rasluiġtheach ar an tí nach bí do láthair; cuirid tú iongnad orm má's ormsa labrann tú mar so; na coinġill ar a labramuid ar n-diaid; is ar theampull a chuirp do labair séision.

backbiter, one who speaks insultingly of a person who is not present; you astonish me if it is of me you speak like that; the conditions which we are going to speak of; it is of the temple of His Body He spoke.

do labair sé go maith ortsa agus rugas buideachas dó air.

he spoke well of you and I thanked him for it.

an dúthaid-si uile air ar
labair me dobeur-sa mé d'a
bur síol; níor labrabair
ormsa an níd fá chóir; do
chionn nár labrabair orm an
níd is ceart; laibeoraid siad
ar glóir do ríogachta, agus
do deunaid caint ar do
neart; laibeoraid mise ar
dathamlacht glóire do mor-
dachta agus ar do gníomaib
iongantacha.

do labairt go haitheasach air;
ag tabairt air labairt ar
mórán do neithib; d'a g-
contrárgad, agus ag labairt
orra go masluigtheach.
ag labairt ar réim chomrad;
creud fá labarthar go holc
orm ar son na neithe fá d-
tugaim buideachas? ar
Eirinn amail adeuram go
grod da éis so.
ℯ. ní aibeora tú olc ré uachtarán
do phobuil; ní epur brithem-
nacht for nech; ní ráidtear
sgeuluigeacht orra go ráng-
adar chugainne; ní ráidtear
sgeul orra.

ní haithristear sgeulaideacht
orra; aithreósdar an ní-si;
ag so an níd aithristear
air; sgeul ar choileach agus
ar tharb d'innisin.
ro innis sí sgeula do ar gach
marbad dá n-deárna D.;
ní tháinic fós neach ar bith
d'foillsiugad ná d'innisin
uilc ar bith ort.

all this land of which I have
spoken I will give to your
seed; ye have not spoken
of me the thing that is
right; for ye have not
spoken of me the thing
which is right; they shall
speak of the glory of thy
kingdom, and talk of thy
power; as for me I will be
talking of the beauty of the
glory of thy majesty and of
thy wondrous works.
to inveigh against him; provoking him to speak of
many things; contradicting
them and speaking insult-
ingly of them.
speaking of the course of
conversation; why am I
evil spoken of for that for
which I give thanks; as we
shall say of Ireland soon
after.
thou shalt not speak evil of
the ruler of thy people; I
pronounce not judgment
on any one; no tidings are
told of them till they
reached us; no tale is told
of them.
no tidings are told of them;
this thing shall be told;
here is what is told of him;
to tell a cock and bull
story.
she told him the tale of all the
slaughter that D. had made;
neither did any one show or
speak any harm of thee.

do foillsiġeaḋ ḋaṁ orraibsi re lucht tíġe Chlóé go ḃ-fuilid inṁreasana eadraiḃ; tá casaoiḋ ḋólásach agus foill-siuġaḋ peacaiḋ ġniḋeas an peacthach air féin lé sagart.

it hath been declared to me of you by them that are of the house of Chloe that there are contentions among you; it is a sorrowful accusation and declaration of sin which the sinner makes against himself to a priest.

foillsíġid féin oruinn cionnas do chuaḋmar asteach chu-guiḃse agus an gleus ar ar fill sibse ó íoḋaluiḃ chum Dé; do chum go nocht fuiḋe smuaintiġ ar ṁórán do chroíḋiḃ.

they themselves show of us how we entered unto you, and how you turned from idols to God; that the thoughts of many hearts may be revealed.

ní cheilfidís gan a nochtaḋ ar ḋaoine ba úirísle ná sin é; níl aon ṁaith ag caint lé claḋaire ar ṁisneach a ġla-caḋ; biaiḋ caint a theanga ar breitheaṁnas.

they would not refrain from revealing it about people humbler than that; there is no use in talking to a coward about taking courage; his tongue will be talking of judgment.

o. canfad mise doḋ' neart.

I will sing of thy power.

ná trácht ar théid san ait 'n ar chroch neach é féin; trácht-muíd ar an g-cóṁráḋ do ḃí againn arís; an eagnuiḋeacht noch thráctas ar na suḃáilciḃ agus ar na lochtaiḃ.

don't speak of a rope in a place where a man hanged himself (15); let us resume our former discourse; the science which treats of virtues and vices.

leabar thráchtas ar luiḃiḃ; leabar thráchtas ar ealaḋain na heagnuíḋeachta; cad é ar a ḃ-fuil sib ag trácht? d'éisḋ sé ris an ní ar a rab-adar ag trácht; do chuala mé trácht air.

a book that treats of herbs; a book which treats of the art of logic; what are you talking of? he listened to what they were talking of; I have heard him spoken of.

ní feudann a chlos trácht ar a beiṫ pósda; tá trácht ar ṡíṫ ann; leabar ar a d-tráchtar ar beatha agus ar bás na mairtíreach.

he can't abide talk about his being married; there is talk of peace; a book which treats of the life and death of martyrs.

neach sgríobas ar na haim-
searaib; sgríobaid Maoise
ar an b-fireuntacht thig ó'n
Reacht.

ní'l staraide dá sgríobann
uirre; an té ar ar sgríob
Maoise annsan Reacht;
do bríg gur gabadar mórán
do láim stair do sgríobad ar
na neithib ag a b-fuil a
sáirfios aguinne.

is leis sin do gríosad mise ré
sgríobad na staire-si ar
Eirionnchaib; mar sgríob-
thar air; mar atá scríobtha
air; a d-tosach an leabair
atá sgríobtha orm.

a g-ceann an leabair atá
sgriobtha ormsa is 'aoibinn
leam do thoil do deanam o
mo Dhiá'; do chuimnigea-
dar go rabadar na neithe-si
sgríobtha air.

cuimnig ar giorra do cháirde
beo (54); cuimnig ar an
uair nach d-tig ar ais; beirim
buídeachas ré mo Dhia
gach uair chuimnigim or-
raibse; cuimnig ormsa an
tan thiocfas tú ad' ríogacht
féin.

cuimnig ormsa an uair beithear
maith agad, agus cuimnig do
Fharaoh me; do chuimnig
mé ar an t-seanaimsir, do
smuain mé ar oibreachaib
do lam; níor chuimnig an
t-áirdfeadmanach air, acht
do dearmuid é; an tan do
chuimnig air féin.

one who writes about the
times; Moses writes of the
righteousness that comes
from the law.

there is no historian (among
those) that write of her;
he of whom Moses wrote in
the law; for as much as
many have taken in hand to
set forth a declaration of the
things which are well known
to us.

it is by that I was incited to
write this history of Irishmen; as it is written of
him; in the beginning of
the book it is written of
me.

at the head of the book it is
written of me, "I am de-
lighted to do thy will O my
God"; they remembered that
these things were written of
Him.

remember how short you
have to live; remember the
hour which does not come
back; I thank my God upon
every remembrance of you;
remember me when thou
shalt come into thy kingdom.

think on me when it shall be
well with thee, and make
mention of me to Pharaoh;
I have remembered the old
time, I have mused upon
the works of thy hands; the
chief butler did not remember him, but forgot him;
when he came to himself.

cuiṁniġ ort féin; an tan chuiṁnígim ar mo ḋéaraiḃ; claonaiḋ sé aignead chum go g-coiṁneóchaḋ air; cuiṁneochaim-ne ar ainm an Tiġearna; dá ḃríġ sin cuiṁneochaḋ ortsa.

recollect yourself; when I am mindful of my tears; he applies his mind to remember it; we will remember the name of the Lord; therefore will I remember thee.

noch do chuiṁniġ orruinn ion ar staid uiríseal; ceangladh mo theanga d'uachtar mo ḃéil muna g-cuiṁniġid mé ortsa; buḋ cóir dúinn cuiṁniuġaḋ ar an t-síorruiḋeacht áḋbail úd; cuiṁniġ mé.[1]

who remembered us in our humble state; let my tongue cleave to the roof of my mouth if I do not remember thee; we should think of that vast eternity; remember me.

do chuiṁniġ mé ar Dhia; cuiṁniġim mo ṡeinm san oiḋche; cuiṁneochaḋ bliaḋna láiṁe deise an té is ró áirde; cuiṁniġ mo díograis dó.

I have thought of my God; I call to remembrance my song in the night; I will remember the years of the right hand of the Most High; remember my kindness to him.

cuiṁneochaiḋ mé cineul grádach an Tiġearna; cuiṁniġ sé na seanlaethe; ní sguirim d'a ḃeith ag coiṁnuiġaḋ oruiḃ um' urnuiġiḃ.

I will mention the loving kindness of the Lord; he remembered the days of old; I cease not making mention of you in my prayers.

smuain ormsa (27).

think of me.

is maith an urnaiġe smuaineaḋ ar an m-bás; is cóir dúinn smuaineaḋ go minic ar luach saothair na ḃ-fíreun; do smuaineaḋ ar an ní atá re teacht; smuainfead ar h-oibreachaiḃ uile, agus ar do ġníoṁarthaiḃ do ḋeunaḋ cuiṁne.

it is a good prayer to think of death; we should think often of the reward of the righteous; to think of the future; I will think of all thy works, and my talking shall be of thy doings.

ag a d-téid an ġlóir a náire

whose glory is in their shame,

---

[1] Cuiṁniġim governs the accusative often; I have got 16 examples.

dóib noch smuaineas ar neithib talṁaide; bíod go b-fuilim bocht agus easbuid-each, smuainid an Tiġearna orm ; an uair chuiṁniġim ort ar mo leabaid, agus annsan oidche faire mar smuainim ort ; *o.* smuainid olc agus do níd é.

an uair smuainim ar saoithib na hEreann; fuaraid sé m'fuil tan smuainim air ; na bíod 'na róchás orraib roiṁe láiṁ creud adeurthaoi agus ná smuainid air ; níl smuainead aige ar urchóid.

níor smuaineas air ; ní smuai-neann sé ar an olc ; gach ógán do smuaineas ar dul lá éigin isan Eaglais ; do ṁeabruġad ar urchóid foili-thiġ ; *a.* aṁail ná saoilead sib far in bethaid.

cealg biasa g-croide na droinge noch smuaineas an t-olc[1] ; agus nír smuain croíde duine na néithe do ullṁuiġ Dia don druing ġráduiġeas é; *o.* do bí mo ṡúile na n-dúsgad a d-tráthaib na hoídche chum smuainiuġad ann do briathraib.

aṁáil ná saoilsad sib for in bethaid.

who mind earthly things ; though I am poor and needy, the Lord careth for me;when I remember thee on my bed, and in the night of watchfulness when I think of thee ; they imagine wick-edness and practise it.

when I think of the nobles of Ireland ; it chills my blood when I think of it ; take no thought beforehand what ye shall speak, neither do ye premeditate ; he means no harm.

I did not intend it ; it thinketh not evil; every youth who thinks of entering one day or other into the Church; to plot secret mischief; as if ye were not thinking of life.

deceit is in the heart of them that imagine evil ; nor have entered into the heart of man the things which God hath prepared for those who love Him ; mine eyes were awake in the night time in order to be occu-pied in thy words.

as if ye were not thinking of life.

---

[1] Smuainim sometimes governs the accusative.

Iarraim, Sírim, Aitchim, Atchuingim, Guidim, Impidim, Aslaigim, etc.

dá ní d'iarr mé ort, ná diúlt iompa mé suil eugfas mé (100); do iarradar air fuireach acu féin; an té saothruigeas, is dó féin saothruigeas sé, óir iarraid a beul air é; do iarradar air imtheacht as a d-tórannaib féin.

two things have I required of thee, deny me them not before I die; they besought Him to abide with them; he who labours, labours for himself, for his mouth craves it of him; they besought Him to depart out of their boundaries.

do iarradar air cómhartha do thaisbeunad ó neam dóib; d'iarrus míle maithfiochas air, fa mar chuireas air feithiom comfad soin; na hiarr orm th'fagbáil nó fillead ó beith ad' leanmuin; iarramuid ar Dhia seilb do glacad air ar g-croíde lé n-a grása ar an t-saogal so; tré a n-glacann sé seilb air ar n-anam.

they asked him to show them a sign from Heaven; I asked him a thousand pardons for making him wait so long; intreat me not to leave thee, or to return from following after thee; we beg of God to take possession of our hearts by his grace in this life; by which it takes possession of our soul.

iarr ormsa gid bé ar bith is áil leat agus dobeura mé duit é; do iarradar air a lám do chur air; do iarradar air buain ris; do iarraidís air cumailt ré himeal a eudaig amáin.

ask me whatever thou wilt, and I will give it thee; they besought him to put his hand upon him; they besought him to touch him; they asked him that they might touch if it were but the border of his garment.

ro gluais sé ag iarraid sgeul ortha; druidid rium, iarraim mar athchuingid oruib; d'iarr sé d'athchuingid air dul leis d'á thig féin; iarramaid fós d'athchuinge orraib gan grás Dé do gábáil chugaib go díomaoin.

he went to ask tidings of them; come near to me, I pray you; he besought him to come into his house; we beseech you also that ye receive not the grace of God in vain.

iarraim d'athchuinge orraib geurchoimeud do deunam daoib ar an muintir thógbas siosma; do sír mé go díthchiollach air teacht chugaib-se; ag sírim ar Dhia gan a ainnéis féin do chur toirmisg ar thíodlaic-ídib Ríg na féile; sírim-se Pól d' athchuinge oruib tré macántas agus ceannsacht Chríost.

I beseech you to be on your guard against those who cause schisms; I earnestly desired him to come unto you; beseeching God that his own unworthiness may not stop the gifts of the king of bounty; I Paul beseech you by the meekness and gentleness of Christ.

sírim-se d'ath-chuinge oraib siúbal daoib mar is iomchubaid don gairm chum ar goiread ib; aitchim ort, deunaid é; aitchim ort, aithris dam creud an ní é; aitchim ort, glac an tabartus chuirim chugad; aitchim ort, éist liom.

I beseech you that ye walk worthy of the vocation wherewith ye are called; pray do it; pray tell me what it is; pray accept the present I send you; pray hear me.

a. in cor-sa conattecht for firu h-Erenn, comlund óenfir, atetha; do athchuingid mé éle mo beul; aon ní amháin d'athchuingid mé ar an Tigearna, ag sin an ní iarrfam; atá sí da athchuinge ort beith díleas dí.

this condition thou requiredst of the men of Ireland, thou mayest take it; I entreated him with my mouth; one thing alone have I desired of the Lord, that I will require; she begs of you to be true to her.

guidim ort[1]; guidim ar Dia; guid orrainn na peacthaig; do guide ar beodaib; *a.* guidim itge for Dia; impigim ar Mhuire Naomtha atá riam na h-óig; impigim ort, a Ríg móir na n-ildúile.

I beseech thee; I pray God; pray for us sinners; to pray for the living; I pray a prayer to God; I beseech the Blessed Mary, ever Virgin; I beseech thee, O great God of the many elements.

do chuir mé d'impide ort.

I besought thee.

gidead cheana tré grád is usa liom impide chur ort.

yet for love's sake I rather beseech thee.

---

[1] Guidim generally takes the accusative.

aslaiġim ort; ar n-a aṡl ach do ríġ Ciannachtá fair; is eiside ra aslaiġ ar Aod an t-innriud deunaṁ; an t-árdchíos éiliġeas sé orruinn; ocus conattacht in n-gae bulga bar Laeg; cuinfed-sa ar an g-Coimdid gairde saogail dó-sam; cuinchis F. for T. cath can chárdi; rochuindich E. a ingen for T.

I beseech you; he being solicited by the king of Ciannachta; it was he who solicited A. to commit this ravage; the tribute He demands of us; and he demanded the *gae bulga* from Laeg; I will beseech the Lord for shortness of life for him; F. demanded from T. a battle without respite; E. asked T. for his daughter.

Fóirim, Cóimeudaim, Cumdaigim, Cosnaim, Imchosnaim, Caomnaim, Díduim, Imdídnim, Saoraim, Inioclann, Sabáilim, Tárthaigim, Aingim.

fóir orruinn; fóir mo ṁíchredeaṁ; d'fóir sé ar dáoiniḃ oile, fóiread sé air féin; go b-fóirid Dia ormsa, ní raiḃ urchóid agam ann; ni b-fuil pinginn aguinn le fóirithin ornn féin; do fóir sé orm a n-Ephesus.

help us, help my unbelief; he saved others, let him save himself; God help me, I meant no harm by it; we have not a penny to help ourselves; he ministered unto me at Ephesus.

a. aingid imdibe ar bibdamnacht Rectto; *o.* anaic leat; *a.* domm anacul ar intledaib; anaicfead ar an pericil úd tú; *a.* rommain ar gabthaib; *o.* éiriġ a Thiġearna agus anaic mé.

circumcision protects us from the condemnation of the Law; take heed; to save me from snares; I will save you from that danger; he protected me from dangers; up Lord and help me.

a. ainsiunn Críst ar cech ernbás ocus ar thein! *o.* cabraid sinn a Dhé ár slánuiġthe; tárthaiġ sinn.

may Christ protect us from every death-by-sword, and from fire; help us O God of our salvation; defend us.

a. Dia dom chobair ar cech guasacht nodguasim; d' furtaiġ orruinn i n-ar n-easbaidib; *o.* cuidiġ-sí liom; *o.* tabair cabair dúinn ó buairead.

coiṁeuduiġ sib féin ar ṁadruiġib; tárla go rabadar a coiṁeud air; go g-coiṁeudfá iad ar olc; ar d-tuigse do choiṁeud ar cheilg an diabail.

chor go g-coiṁeudfuid thú ar an mnaoi spleaduiġeas; chum é féin do choiṁeud ar pheacad; bidid ar bur g-coiṁeud ar na daoinib; coiṁeudad an fear faisnéise é féin ar rún díoġaltais.

cuṁdaiġ mé ar neart an ḃaintéir agus ar innlib lucḣta oibriġthe na h-urchóide; d'á chuṁdach ar easarluiġeacht nó ar aicíd; chum a g-cuṁduiġthe ar aththuitim thiobuisdiġ.

cosnaid sinn ar na spioradaib neaṁġlana; chum go g-coiseónfuide iad ar chuṁachtaib an diabail; ag cosnaṁ chrioslaiġ agus chuain na críche ar foirneart na Scot; *o.* coiseonaid tú mé ó buaidread; ionnus go b-feudfad é féin d'imchosnaṁ ar lot na luchóg úd.

caoṁain orainn féin inn; *a.* corob é caeṁna dorónsat for na piastaib; eangacḣ

help us; God to help me against every danger that I risk; he relieved us in our wants; be thou my help; help us against tribulation.

beware of dogs; it came to pass that they watched him; that thou shouldst keep them from evil; to guard our understanding against the wiles of the devil.

that they may keep thee from the woman that flatters; to keep himself from sin; beware of men; let the informer beware of the desire of revenge.

keep me from the force of the snare and from the traps of the wicked doers; to preserve him from incantation or disease; to preserve them from fatal relapse.

they defend us from the impure spirits; that they may be defended against the power of the devil; defending the frontier and shore of the country against the violence of the Irish; thou shalt preserve me from trouble; that he may be able to defend himself against the hurt of those mice.

save us from ourselves; and it was the remedy they invented against the reptiles;

do churthar ar chapull d'a chaoṁnad ar chuilid.

a net which is put on a horse to protect him from flies.

nosditnifit a n-almsana for thenid brátha; níor feudaid iad féin do ṡairdídion air; *a.* sciath Dé dom dítin ar intledaib demna ; gan aon díon ar dúr-doininn.

their alms shall protect them from the fire of doom ; they could not protect themselves from it ; God's shield to guard me against the snares of demons ; without any protection against the hard weather.

gan díon ar ġaoith nó ar ġairbṡín; chum na soiġdiuiríġe do díon ar an náṁuid ; óir fa dearb leo nach b-fuil ní 'san m-bith is mó chaoṁnas agus doġní dídean do n' duine ar díbfeirg Dé do thuilleaṁ ; ar chor gur ab móide do feudfad é féin d' imdídean agus d' anacul air.

without shelter against wind or rough weather ; to protect the soldiers from the enemy; for they were certain that there is nothing in the world better guards and protects a man from meriting the anger of God ; so that he might be able to defend and protect himself against it.

saor inn ó olc, .i. ár saorad ar an uile olc ; dot' ṡaorad ar an mnaoi coiṁthiġid, noch ṁeallas le n-a briathraib ; saor é ar dul síos annsa pholl ; atá tu saor ar aní is toil leat do deunaṁ.

deliver us from evil, *i.e.* deliver us from all evil ; to deliver thee from the strange woman who flatters with her words; deliver him from going down to the pit; you are free to do as you please.

atá mise saor ar a deunad nó léigean dó; *a.* guidmit-ne tusa co ra ṡaera sinn for a n-ulcu ; *a.* co ro saerit for dígail Dé ; é féin d'inioclann ar ṁil m-bréige na beathad so.

I am free to do it or let it alone ; we pray thee that thou deliver us from their evils ; that they were saved from the vengeance of God ; to guard oneself against the false honey of this life.

neach do ṡábáil ar a ġabáil ; neach do ṡábáil ar urchóid ; neach do ṡábáil féin ar díobáil ; ní'l neart nó sábáil air ; ní'l neart agam

to save a person from being taken ; to save one from harm ; to indemify oneself; there is no help for it ; I have just enough to preacht oiread go díríoch do sábálad ar báslé gortain mé.

chum a d-tárthála ar aththuitim ; o. do thárthaiġ tusa sinn ó ar náimdib; a. domm' imdegail ar neim, ar loscud, ar badud, ar guin ; a. dia himdegail forra ; fuasgail orm ; fuasgail ar mo buidin ; fuasgail m'anam.

chum ar n-admála umla ar na tairbeada dobeir Críost dúinn do chur a g-céill ; ag agart ar gach neach furtacht do thabairt dó ; ná'r agrad Dia an choir sin ort ; ná'r agrar orra é.

a. gan an Bhoruma d'agrad orra ; a. airisiom for an m-breith sin ; aisim air, atá ais agam air ; ag aithe fair inna n-dearna d'ulc fri tuaith ocus eacclais ; aithfeoraid sé oruib.

ní ro airigsium fort áilcius dula dochum nime ocut ; do ariġ sí ar a corp féin go raib sí slán ; d'aithin sé ormsa nachar b'amudán mé.

aithniġthear an crann ar a thorad ; aithneocham é ar ar n-deaġ-oibrib ; aithniġim-se é ar a ġuth ; a. atotath-gén ar do thuarascbáil; is lia aithne ar oinmid ioná aithnigeas sisi cách.

atá aithne agam ort ad' ainm ; a. co n-a eladain ar dul do

serve myself from death.

to preserve them from relapse ; thou hast saved us from our enemies ; to protect me from poison, from burning, from drowning, from wounding ; to protect her from them ; relieve me ; relieve my company ; deliver my soul.

to signify our humble acknowledgment of the benefits Christ confers on us ; importuning every one to give him help ; that God may not avenge that crime on you; let it not be laid to their charge.

not to demand the Borumean tribute from them ; to abide by that decision ; I depend on or confide in him ; revenging on him the evils he had committed against the laity and the Church ; he will reprove you.

we did not perceive by thee that thou hadst a desire of going to heaven ; she knew by her body that she was healed ; he found by me that I was no fool.

the tree is known by its fruit ; we shall know it by our good works ; I know him by his voice ; I recognised you by a description of you ; more know Jack-pudding than Jack-pudding knows.

I know thee by name ; at their learning (when they learned)

Chonall; a Dhé, ag ar beatha síorruide eolas fírinneach do beith ort; níor b'áil dó sochuide d'a fios fair; *a.* ro fess orthu.

that Conall was going; O God, whom truly to know is everlasting life; he did not wish many to know this about him; it was known about them; they were found out.

ná fionnad a h-athair fuirre, agus na fergaided an t-athair fria; tuigfid tú ormsa ar gach aon nós gurb mé d'óglach úmal; ní fiú dúib tréithe nó laige do thuigsin dúinne foraib.

that her father might not discover her crime and that the father should not be vexed with her; you shall find by me on all occasions that I am your humble servant; it is not worthy for you, that we should perceive dastardliness and weakness in you.

nar chomaillis na timnai ro aithin Dia fort do chomét; *a.* aithris for céill; sgribneoir nach d-tugann d'a aire acht aoir ag amusdraig ar chách amail madaig; neach anas ar deirid cuideachtan (8).

that you have not fulfilled the commands which God commanded you to keep; return to sense or reason; a writer who cares only to criticize and bark at every one as a dog; one who lags behind a company.

a. anfad-sa fair; níor féd fuirech fair; *a.* arcelith ar chách; *a.* argain Coirpri ar saer-chlannaib hErenn; *a.* ro arraid orra .i. ruc orra; *a.* astartaig M. forro; *a.* asruluus airi.

I will stand to it, abide by it; he could not abide or stand it; ye rob every one; Coirpre's slaughter of the free clans of Ireland; he overtook them; M. overtook them; I escaped from him.

a. athél ar ocht ocus gorti; cia an t-úgdar ar a b-fuil tú ag athchagnad; do bagair se teinid agus cloideam orra; do bagair sé orra gan innsead d'éinneach dá thaob féin; do bí do dánacht ann bagar ar an g-críochsmacht;

I shall die of misery and hunger; what is that author you are chewing the cud upon; he threatened them with fire and sword; he charged them that they should tell no man of him; he dared to menace the government;

bagruiġthear ar Fharao bás a chéidġeinti.

ro bói sí ag béim for a fer 'man maoraiġeacht do rad d'Finachta ; gur beanad binneán Chiaráin air.

mór do ḃen t'ég orm-sa ; a. ro gellsat a cluic acus a m-bachla do bein fair ; is ar amadánacht beathuiġthear beul na n-amadán ; gurb ar a phearsoin atáid ag braith.

atáim ag brath ort ; do ḃí an ciontach ag brath orm chum mo ṁillte; atá an pheannaid cheudna ag brath ort-sa ; ní'l siad ag brath an dadaṁ oruinne ; tá sé brath ar a bualad.
dá m-beith breathnuġad againn orruinn féin ní ḃeurthaoi breath orruinn ; breathnuiġ arís air; breathnuġad go glinn ar ní; breathnuiġ go grinn air.
breathnuiġeam go grinn air; breathnuġad ar ġníoṁ do réir a chinneaṁna ; is coír daṁ an breathnuġad-sa do beith agam orraiḃ uile.
brisid sé a druim ar dó ; do brisead amach ar sgaoil ; an tan do bris mé na cúig aráin ar na cúig ṁíle ; ná bris an bata so orm ; ná cuir-se d'fiachaiḃ orm síth

Pharaoh was threatened with the death of his first-born.
she reproached her husband about the stewardship he had given to Finachta ; that Ciarán's bell was struck against him, i.e. he was excommunicated.
much has your death touched me ; they threatened to strike their bells and croziers against him, i.e. to excommunicate him ; the mouth of fools feeds on foolishness ; that they are aimed at his person.
I have a design, dependence, expectation, on you ; the ungodly laid wait for me to destroy me ; the like punishment attends you ; they are not expecting anything from us ; he is about to beat him.
if we would judge ourselves we should not be judged ; try it again, look at it again; to peep at a thing ; observe it sharply.

let us consider it attentively ; to judge of an act by its result ; it is meet for me to think this of you all.

he breaks his back in two ; to get loose ; when I broke the five loaves among the five thousand ; don't break my stick ; do not force me to break the peace with him :

H

do brisead air; an síth dob áil riot brisead orm-sa ?

would you fain break the peace ?

dá m-brised in buanna ar an tiġearna fa gan anṁain aige in athráithe; ro bris an phláiġ asteach orra; a. brisis Macha forru; tátham gur brisead leis in ríġ ar a náṁaid.

if the buony should disappoint the lord by not remaining with him a full quarter; the plague was great among them; Macha vanquished them; we find that the king defeated the enemy.

brisid go hobann cath ar bur náimdib; a. do briseadar Cenél Conaill cath forru; do bris sé trí catha orra; ro bris D. maidm ar Ghallaib.

suddenly overthrow your foes; the Cenél Conaill defeated them; he broke three battalions of them, or, won three battles against them; D. defeated the English.

ar m-brisead madma forra; a. do chlod cath for Cormac; cathraoinead ré M. for L.; éiriġ, uṁluiġ thú féin, agus mar sin buaideochaid tú ar do charaid.

when they were defeated; who gained a battle over Cormac; a battle was gained by M. over L.; go, humble yourself and thus you make sure of your friend.

a. buaid sé an choill; do buaddar orainn go fírinnioch obann; do buaid mise breis na haimsire air; do buaid sé ort; do buaid sé air; buaidfid mise ortsa; do buaidiomar orra; níor feudadar buaduġad uirre.

he (the fox) gains the wood; they gained upon us apace; I gained the advantage of time upon him; he excelled you; he got the better of it; I shall get the better of you; we got the wind of them; they could not prevail against her.

buaid do breith ar an náṁaid; is missi buadaigfes de bar mac n-Damáin mic Dáre.

to vanquish the enemy; it is I that shall triumph therein over the son of Damán son of Dáre.

leis sin do ṁadmaid a bean amach ar deoraib; ro maid a faitbiud gáire fair.

with that his wife burst out into tears; he burst into a fit of laughter at him.

maidid forra; do muiġead an cath ar Chonnachtaib; do muiġead a ġean gaire air; ro maid re macaib an ríġ

he defeats them; the battle was won against the Connachtmen; he fell to laughing, broke out laughing;

ar an chath sin.

do máiḋead ar Gallaib; maiḋm le Gaoiḋil ar Ghallaib; *a.* rogab maiḋm for U; ar maiḋm forra; ra fail inti conmae foraib in cath-sa don chur-sa.

a. do rain O. cath forru; *a.* is leo do rained cath for D. for rig Temrach; ro sraoinead for Ghallaib; ro sraoinead ar an tóraiḋ; *a.* ro sraeinead an cath forrtha.

do brostuiġeas é ar aġaiḋ le geallaṁnacha breáġacha; d'a m-brostuġaḋ air éision do ġabáil chuca; ní tú brostuiġeas orm na clanna; do bruachaḋ ar aġaiḋ; atá daoine dosgúḋacha do bruḋas asteach ar ḋaoine gnóthuiġeacha; cáirdeas do bruġaḋ air.

do bualaḋ air; do buaileadar orainn go dásachtach; imthiġ do bealach, nó buailfead-sa ort; do buail ormsa go truailliġe; buail le clochaib air; buailfiḋear beagán air; buailtear cos air.

do buail sé bas ar Iosa; do buaileaḋ buille do chasúr air ann a chliabán; buille do bualaḋ ar an ngiall ar neach; cleas do bualaḋ air; do buail sé droichleas air: dorna do bualaḋ air; preab do chois do bualaḋ san tóin ar neach.

preab do bualaḋ ar neach; is

the sons of the king defeated that battalion.
the foreigners were defeated; a defeat of the English by the Irish; he defeated U; when they were defeated; he is here who will win the battle against them this time.

O. defeated them; by them was gained a battle over D. king of Tara; the English were defeated; the pursuer was defeated; they were beaten.

I egged him on with fair promises; exhorting them to receive him; it is not you that excite the clans against me; to coast along; there are impertinent persons who break in on men of business; "to get in with him."

to attack him; they fell upon us desperately; go your way, or else I will fall upon you; he fell foul of me; stone him; he shall receive few stripes; he is kicked.

he gave Jesus a slap; he got a knock of a hammer in his cradle, *i.e.* is a born fool; to give one a blow on the cheek; to jest with him; he played him a bad trick; to buffet him; to give a person a kick.

to give one a jerk; I must

éigean daṁsa speach do
bualaḋ air ; go m-buailiḋ
Dia uireasbaiḋ ort ; neach
do greaḋbualaḋ ar a thao-
baiḃ ; do ḃuail sé ar reacht
gâiríḋe ; do ḃualaḋ amach
ar anchaithioṁ ; do ḃualaḋ
amach ar iomurca do ráḋ.

have a fling at him ; may
God afflict you with poverty;
to strike a person on his
sides ; he fell to laughing ;
to lash out into expense,
to lash out into expressions.

tug C. fa ḋeara ann sin trí naoi
g-ceoláin do ḃuain **ar**
Chonall ; airgiod do ḃuain
amach ar imirt.

then C. caused thrice nine
little bells to be rung against
Conall ; to win money at
play.

o. atá mo theanga **ag cailli-**
oṁuin orm ; atá mo chroiḋe
ag caillioṁuin orm ; atá mo
neart ag caillioṁuin orm ;
caillfeaḋ ort ; **an** drong
chailleas ar an **marḃ** chuireas comniaoin orra.

my tongue fails me ; my heart
fails me ; my strength fails
me ; I shall fail thee ; those
who fail (or neglect) the
dead person that confers a
favour on them.

caillim a g-coṁnuiḋe ar char-
tada ; liathróid do chaill ar
tenis ; do chaitheas an ṁaid-
in go hiomlán timchioll air ;
cloch do chaithioṁ air ;
do thosuiġ sé ag cathaḋ
droichṁeasa ar gach madaḋ
eile a g-comórtus leis féin.

I always lose at cards ; "to
brickoll." (to lose a ball at
tennis) ; I spent the whole
morning about it ; to fling
a stone at him ; he began
to show contempt for every
other dog in comparison
with himself.

mórán saothair do chaitheaṁ
ar obair ; chor go g-caith-
fidís go foluiġtheach ar an
b-fíreun a g-croiḋe; crann
tábaill chum lámach cloch
ar náṁuid ; láthraiḋ Cú
cloich m-big for na héonu.

to bestow much pains on a
work ; that they may privily
shoot at the true of heart ;
a sling to shoot stones at
an enemy ; Cu throws a
small stone at the birds.

ná teilg ar siubal mé; neach
do theilgean ar agaiḋ a slíġe
a chaillte; tilg oirre[1];tilgeaḋ
é a chiad chlach oirre[1] ; do
theilg neull soillseach sgáile
orra.[1]

cast me not away ; to hurry
one along on the road of
destruction ; fire at her (the
duck) ; let him fling the
first stone at her ; a bright
cloud overshadowed them.

---

[1] *Scotch.*

snáth do chasad ar a chéile;
mór liach ro ceacht ar an t-
sluaiġ; mar a n-abair gur ab
é am fá 'r cheangail an cíos
sin uirre; do cheannach ar
cáirde.

an fírinne do cheilt air; ní
cheilfead sgeula ort; ceilid
sé a ġrása ar na daoinib
deismireacha; ceiltear uimir
a bliadan don bruidteach.

guidim thú ná ceil orm an ní
fiafróchas mé díot; do beith
ceilte nó falaiġthe ort;
folaiġ mé ar chomhairle na
n-drochdaoine, ó chogad
luchta oibriġthe na hur-
chóide; creud fá b-folchann
tú th'agaid orm?

níor folchad m'osnada ortsa;
do rachainn a b-folach air;
méid atái-siu ac céssacht
formsa.

ar g-cinniod ar an g-cómhairle
sin dóib; as í cómhairle ar
ar cinnead aca; is é
cómhrac ar ar chinneadar—
cómhrac croibneartmhar do
deunam; do chin sí ar
mnáib a comhaimsire i sgéim;
dias do chinn ar méid agus
ar maise ar chách; triúr
do chinn ar iathaib-sean.

do chlaonadar air; d'eagla
go g-claonfaidis breithe-
amhnas ar aoinneach a m-
buaidread; do chlaonad air.

to twist thread; great grief
came over the army; where
he says that that was the
time he imposed that tri-
bute on her; to buy on
trust.

to hide the truth from him;
I will not conceal the stories
or facts from you; he hideth
his graces from the curious;
the number of his years is
hidden to the oppressor.

hide not from me, I pray thee,
the thing that I shall ask
thee; to be concealed or
hidden from you; save me
from the counsel of the
wicked, from the war of
mischief makers; why hidest
thou thy face from me?

my groaning has not been hid
from you; I would fain have
gone to hide from him;
much as thou art reproach-
ing me.

when they had determined on
that counsel or plan; this
is the counsel on which
they fixed; the combat they
fixed upon was—to do a
stronghand fight; she sur-
passed all the women of her
time in beauty; two who
excelled all in bulk and
beauty; three who ruled
their lands.

deceived him, were false
to him; lest they should
pervert the judgment of
anyone in affliction; to rely
upon him or it.

do chlaonaḋ a ınntinne ar ní.

do chlis me ort ; do chlis-chealg sé ar a thír ; cia hé so ar a g-cluinim a léithéide so ? do ḃríǵ go g-cualaiḋ sé mórán air ? do chualaiḋ mé ó ṁórán ar an ḃ-fear so ; creud é so do chluinim ort ?

do chualadar ortsa go d-teagas-gann tú do chách Maoise do thréigean ; grása iarraiḋ air chum coiṁniǵthe ar a g-cualaiḋ ; coiṁniǵthear orra is an Aifrionn ; an tan do choiṁniǵmíd-ne orra ar talaṁ.

cuimsiuǵaḋ ar gach teagṁus ; cóiriǵ mé ar m' eascaraid ; tuataḋ .i. neach do choṁ-nuiǵeas ar tuaith ; ar son nár chongaiṁ duine ar bith ar tuarasdal sinn ; do chon-gnuiṁ air féin.

a. bás n-aill conutecht forru ; atá armáil na naṁad ag corruiǵe ar n-aǵaiḋ ; corruiǵ ort ; is fad ó do ḃí sé ag cratha le n-a theangaiḋ ar an g-críochsmacht ; ra chrechtnaiǵ cach díb bar araile ; do chraobsgaoileaḋ air.

do chromaḋ ar aithrisgeul neithe éigin d'innsin ; do chromaḋ ar chómrac ; do chromaḋ ar ǵul ; do chromaḋ ar obair ; gan cromaḋ ar ṁínscoith.

crosaim ort ; an t-uball so do ḃí crosta orra ; d'feudfainn mo cheann do chrothaḋ

to give his mind to a thing.

I nicked you ; he betrayed his country ; who is this of whom I hear such things ? because he had heard many things of him ; I have heard by many of this man ; what is this that I hear of thee ?

they have heard of thee that thou teachest all to forsake Moses ; to beg His grace to retain what he heard ; a commemoration is made of them in the Mass ; when we celebrate their memory on earth.

a record of every event ; avenge me of mine enemy ; peasant, *i.e.*, one that lives in the country ; because no man has hired us ; he re-frained himself.

another death has been pre-pared for them ; the enemy's army moves forward ; hurry on ; he had long brand-ished his tongue against the government ; each of them inflicted wounds on the other ; to tell about him.

to launch out with the recital of something ; to fall to fighting ; to begin to cry , to fall to work ; without stooping to find a flower.

I forbid you ; this apple which was forbidden them ; I could shake my head at

oruiḃ; saiḋḃrios do chruinn-
iuġad ar ṁuin a chéile;
cruthaiġ ormsa.

you; to heap up treasure;
prove to me or for me.

do chruithiġ air é; coir do
cruthnuġaḋ air; cumaisg
ael air; *a.* ro chumasg sé
for in sluag; *a.* ní daresait
ort.

he proved it against him; to
fasten a crime upon him;
mix lime with it; he con-
fused the host; they will
not tell you (or on you?)

dearcaḋ sé ar ṁórḋacht agus
ar ṁaith Dé; daoine do
ġearraḋ 'na mírinniḃ noch
nach láṁfaḋ dearcaḋ orra
idir an ḋá súil; ag grindearc-
aḋ ar an seun agus ar an
sonas do chuaiḋ sé re ollṁu-
ġaḋ fá chóṁair na ḃ-fireun;
atá súile an Tiġearna ann
gach uile ball ag feuchain
ar an olc agus ar an maith;
rachaiḋ mé d'feuchain air.

let him consider the majesty
and goodness of God; to
cut men in pieces who durst
not look them in the face;
contemplating the happi-
ness and bliss which he is
gone to prepare for the
just; the eyes of the Lord
are in every place, beholding the evil and the good;
I will go see him.

an lá thiucfas mé d'feuchain
orra, leanfaiḋ mé a ḃ-peacaḋ
orra; do ḃríġ gur feuch sé
ar uṁla a banóglaiġe féin;
atá ḃeith ag feuchain ar
Dhia aġaiḋ ar aġaiḋ; ar n-
gérfeuchain do Phól ar an
g-cóṁairle.

on the day when I will visit
them, I will visit their sin
upon them; for He hath
regarded the lowliness of
His handmaiden; it is to
see God face to face; Paul
earnestly beholding the
council.

feuchaiḋ ormsa agus biaḋ
iongnaḋ oruiḃ agus leagaiḋ
bur láṁ ar bur m-beul;
feuchain ar neach san
eudan; *o.* d'feuchain ann
m'eudan; feuch orm na
búta so; feuch orm na
bróga so; féuch ort iad.

mark me and be astonished
and lay your hand upon your
mouth; to look one in the
face; to look me in the face;
try these boots on me; try
these shoes on me; try
them on (to see if they fit).

o. creud é sin dúinne? feuch
féin dó sin; feudaim mo
chnáṁa uile d'áireaṁ, do
chíd siad agus aṁaircid
orm.

what is that to us? see you to
that; I may count all my
bones, they stare and look
at me.

amairc le truaiġe ar thuirse ar g-croideaḋ ; *a.* t'fairc-siu for nach ní atchifitheá ; bí an drochduine ag faire ar an b-fíreun, agus iarraiḋ a chur chum báis.

in pity behold the sorrow of our hearts ; thy examination of whatsoever thou shouldst see ; the bad man sees the just, and seeks to put him to death.

fédaid cat dercaḋ for ríġ.

a cat can look at a king.

inneosad duit an ní d'imthiġ thart ar mod go saoilfir thú féin ad' fiadnuise súl air ; is iomad gron do chíthear ar an duine bocht.

I shall so express to you what has passed that you will fancy yourself an eye witness ; many a defect is seen in a poor man.

ní ḋeargann arm ortha ; deithfríġ ort, teith ann súd ; greas ort, greasuiġ ort !

weapon does not wound them ; haste thee, escape thither ; make haste, hasten.

na cuile do díbeirt ar siuḃal ; *a.* nimthomoltid do dígail forru ; díġeóltar ort go follus é ; ar a díoġail ort ; díoġail clann Israel ar na Midianachaib.

to drive away the flies ; do not urge me to punish them ; you shall be manifestly punished for it ; to avenge it on you ; avenge the children of Israel on the Midianites.

cá meud ar ar díolais é ? díolaim an móin fichead fód ar phingin ; a ġrása do diúltaḋ orm ; bí dúil againn do ġnáth san níd bíos ag a diúltaḋ orairn ; do ṡeun sé go h-iomlán ormsa é.

for how much did you sell it ? I sell the turf at twenty sods a penny ; to refuse me His grace ; we wish for a thing which is denied us ; he flatly denied it to me.

d'éimiḋ sé go hiomlán ormsa é ; adnacul críostaṁuil d'éimioḋ ar neach ; do doirtiḋ sé a miann ar fóġlaim ; dóirtiḋ sé é féin ar uile saorbronntas a chéadfaḋa.

he flatly denied it me ; to refuse Christian burial to a person ; he devotes himself to learning ; he indulges himself in all the gratifications of his senses.

a. ro dolbestar for alailiu ; *a.* ní doluigim airibsi ; fobith to-n-aidbecht forro a síd ; *a.* isindi dosich a peccad for cách.

they rushed at each other ; the thing which I forgive you, or forgive for you ; because he broke up their fairy mound ; in this (whereas) he tells his sin to everyone.

an dorus do drud air, gan a léigean asteach ; do druid sé an dorus orm ; do druid sé air astiġ ; druideam air ar n-aġaid ; gur dúin sé ar Eoin a b-priosún.

do dúnad oruinn chum an chreidiṁ do bí ré haġaid a ṡoillṡiġthe ; do iadadar ar iomarcuid éisg ionnus gur briseaḋ a líon.

a. atá leusom di forcrid a n-dudesta airibsi ; ná heagair an peacaḋ so orra.

cad é ar ég sé ; cad é ar eug sé ? gideaḋ muna n-déarna mé aoinní do na neithib-si éiliġid siad orm, ní feudann aon duine mo thíodlacaḋ dóiḃ ; ní héidir leo na neithe-si atáid siad d'éiliuġad orm anois a chruthúġad ; *o.* má tá olc ar bith annsa b-fear so éiliġid siad é.

d'éirġe suas air ; aṁail ná éirġead C. air ; ro choiṁéi-riġ cách ar amus a chéile ; eitillfid sé ar siuḃal aṁuil aisling ; ra erail an díomus orra iomraṁ rempa.

is í-síde ra erail foirne a ḃaḋud ; ag erail ar a ṁuintir aḋrad na n déc ; ro iorailettur siad fair-side dola ar amus na Lochlann ; ic a n-uráil for anmandaiḃ na pecdach.

amal dosfurail Dia féin er Moysi ; amal ro eráil Isu forru ; d'furáil sé air ; ro furáil sé air an t-Iarla do

to shut the door against him ; not to let him in ; he shut the door upon me ; he shut him in ; let us draw near ; that he shut up John in prison.

we were shut up unto the faith which should after-wards be revealed ; they en-closed a multitude of fish so that their net broke.

they possess in abundance what is wanting to you ; lay not this sin to their charge.

what did he die of? but if I have not done any of these things whereof they accuse me, no man may deliver me unto them ; they cannot prove the things whereof they now accuse me ; if there be any wickedness in this man let them accuse him.

to affront him ; as C would not rise against him; all rose up against each other ; he shall fly away as a dream ; their pride induced or urged them to row on.

it is she who ordered us to drown him; ordering his people to worship the gods ; they requested him to go to the Lochlanns ; setting them (the dogs) at the souls of sinners.

as God himself enjoined it on Moses ; as Jesus enjoined on them ; he commanded him ; he instigated him to

ṁarbaḋ ; ra furâil forra agus ar cách uile léirthionól do ḋeunam d'innsoiġiḋ Laiġen do thobach na boruṁa forra ; hó arroraill for C. aní fa haccobar leis ; is breallân an ténach n-glacfaḋ airgeaḋ do furáileochaḋ air ; atá Dia ḋa' foráileaḋ féin oruib aṁuíl ar chloinu.

murder the earl ; he commanded them and all in general to assemble and invade the Leinstermen to exact the boruma from them ; when he had imposed on C. what he wished ; a fool is he who would not take money that would be offered to him ; God dealeth with you as with sons.

a. d'fáidiud ar cend Conchu-laind.

to send for Cuchulainn.

a. fáidis teachta ar a cend ; ro fóideastar P. cursúir .i. giolla turuise, for ceann Iosa go n-Gaililée.

he sent a messenger for him ; P. sent a messenger for Jesus to Galilee.

má d'faillid an t-airgead oruib ; is measa liom fir Erenn d'faisnéis ort an oidche rugais Grainne riot ó Theaṁraiġ.

if money fail you ; it grieves me more that the men of Erin should have witnessed thee the night thou tookest Gráinne from Tara.

ní iarann sé ar ní ar bith ; is olc faras bróg chuṁaing ar chois frithir ; atá an bróg so ag fásgaḋ orm ;do feall a theanga air ; ní feallfa mé ort.

it does not fit or suit at all ; it is not fit for anything ; a tight shoe ill fits a sore foot ; this shoe squeezes me ; his tongue failed him ; I will not deceive, or fail you.

a. ar fellad d'A. fair ; mairg feallas ar a charaid ; d'feallaḋ air ; do meallaḋ é nó do feallaḋ air.

A. having failed him, acted treacherously towards him ; woe to him who deceives his friend ; to assassinate him ; he was deceived.

ní biaiḋ náire ar an lucht feitheas ormsa ; do féith mé oruib agus ní raib aon agaib do chlaoi Iob ná thug freagra ar a briathraib.

they shall not be ashamed that wait for me ; I attended unto you and behold there was none of you that convinced Job or that answered his words.

creud ar a b-fuilim ag feitheaṁ ?

what am I looking for ?

ortsa bím ag feitheaṁ ar
fead an laoi ; meathaiḋ mo
ṡúile ag feitheaṁ ar focal
th' fíreuntachta ; atámaoid
ag feithioṁ ar do chineul
grâdach, a Dhé, a lár do
theampuill.
feith ar an Tiġearna agus
tairtheochaiḋ sé thú ; do
rinneas cóṁairle fada ó ṡoin
feithioṁ ort ag do thiġ ;
feith ar an Tiġearna, bí
láidir, agus neartóchaiḋ sé
do chroiḋe, agus deun feitheaṁ ar an Tiġearna.
bí a ṡúil ag feithioṁ ris an
maidin ; do ḋul d'fiaḋach ar
eunlaith ; eunlaitheoir, an
tí doġníḋ fiaḋach ar eun-
laith ; fialġabaiḋ sé é ar a
bórd ; a. focheird ár mór
forru.
an lucht bias ag fochṁuid ar
chreidioṁ tuillid a g-cóṁ-
arthaḋa le hamuiḋeacht ;
fonasc latt ar Morand ; cuir
do chrios ort agus friotháil
ormsa; ag frítheolaṁ ar na
trí féinnidib.
ni láṁfar fuiliuġaḋ iná foir-
ḋeargaḋ ort ; go b-fuadui-
ġeann bás anapuid ar siubal
iad ; an té fanas a b-fad
amuiġ, fuaraiḋ a chuiḋ air ;
a. ní fuirmi nech dimiccim
foir-som.
an tan ro ġeallaisi neṁ do
ġaid form ; na gatad Dia n-
airi ; a. in gét a bullu ar
Crist ?

I look to thee the whole day
long ; my eyes are wasting
looking for the word of thy
righteousness ; we have
thought of thy loving kindness, O God, in the midst
of thy temple.
wait on the Lord and he shall
save thee ; I intended long
ago to wait upon you at
your house ; wait on the
Lord, be strong and He
shall strengthen thine heart,
and wait on the Lord.

his eye waits for the morning ;
to go hunting birds, fowling;
a bird-catcher, he who hunts
birds ; he entertains him at
his table ; he puts great
slaughter on them.

those who joke about religion
deserve to be branded for
folly ; pledge Morand to
thyself ; gird thyself and
serve me ; attending on the
champions.

none will dare to cut or wound
you ; till an untimely death
snatches them away ; he
who remains long out his
dinner grows cold ; let not
anyone despise him.

when you promised to take
heaven from me ; let him
not steal God from him ;
shall I rob Christ of his
members ?

a. ní geṫte na breṫemnachta becca erriu ; dogniat gait er Dia.

a n-gearánann sí ar ṫinneas fiacal ? an drong ag a b-fuil a peacaide ag gearán ar a g-coinsíos; a Ṡaul, creud fá a b-fuil tú ag gérleanṁuin orm ? do ṫógadar gérlean-ṁuin ar Ṗól.

cábla do ġearraḋ ar a ḋó; gearram ar an n-déiġil; do ġleusas orm chum siúbail; maille le rún do ġnóḋuġaḋ air ; ná bíḋiḋ ag gnúsach-taiġ air a chéile.

ná goilleaḋ an ní sin ort; is ró-ṁór do ġoilleas ar mo chroiḋe fearg do chur ort; ní ġoilleann orm a b-fuaras do ṫrioblóid; creud ġoilleas ort; creud ġoilleas ar do ṡúil ? níʼl éin ní orm ; do ġoilleaḋar na saíġdeoi-riḋe air go ġeur agus do chaitheaḋar air.

ionnas go n-greamóchaidís ar a chóṁrád ; níor feudaḋar greamuġaḋ ar a briathra; greas ort, ma tá ; ro greiss a ṁuinntir go diocra for na Lochlannaib; suiḋiḋ sí ar gur ar uiġe.

áit a m-bíd ar g-cur ar a n-eunacha óga ; *a.* no ícaḋ ar cach n-galar; caithfiḋ mé íoc ar mo chartaḋa ; cad é ar íoc tú air ? *a.* cen imaccal-laim forru.

biaiḋ siad ag iomaiṫbear orra féin ; ro baoi an rí ag iom-

---

ye should not defraud them of the petty judgments; they steal from God.

does she complain of tooth-ache? they whose consci-ences are by sin accused; Saul, why persecutest thou me? they raised a persecu-tion against Paul.

to cut a cable in two; let us cut for deal (at cards); I got ready to walk; with a resolution to profit by it; murmur not one against the other.

let not that thing trouble you; I am heartily sorry for having offended Thee; I don't grudge my pains; what ails you? what ails your eye? nothing ails me; the archers have sorely grieved him and shot at him.

that they might catch or take hold of his words; they could not take hold of his words; hurry then; he vehemently excited his people against the Loch-lanns; she is hatching eggs.

a place where they sit on their young birds; it healed (or protected) against every disease; I must pay for my cards; what did you pay for it? without challenging them.

they shall be rebuking them-selves; the King was

chaoined fair ; do iomluit
sé leac ar dorus an tuama ;
do badar ag ingilt ar léana ;
ag innliugad air.
téidid M. agus A. d'ionnsaigid
ar Fharao ; ionnsaig Phát-
raic for chléir Ulad ;
sloigead mór le Niall co n-a
chloinn d'ionnsaigid for
Gallaib ; a. in tain no m-bíu
oc irbáig airib ; ro iordarcaig
sé for Eirinn.

a. la irnigdi airib ; a. ro
laiset a tech for a cend ; a.
do ralá hé for caiseal na
cille ; ní lámfar fuiliugad
ort ; ro lancc in sennín
fort.

do leag sé a m-bóird ar lár ;
sraith do leagad ar thír ; do
lean sé iad, nó orra ; gan
leanamuin orra níos faide ;
leanfaid mé a b-peacadorra ;
do leau Iob ar a samlugad.

leanfuidear a b-fuil ar an g-
cinead so ; atá a fuil d'a
leanmuin oruinn ; do beith
ag sírleanmuin ar ní ; do
lean sí D. ar a lorg ; ní
léigthear ar aon n duine do
chuir. . . .

doléig ar lár focal nó a dó ; do
léigeas ar lár m' uairfaire ;
do léigean ar lár ; do léig sé
ar lár é ; an tan do léigeas
a leas ar cáirde.

léig é ar a rian féin ; do léigean ar sgaoil ; léigfid uile
ar a n-glúinib iad ; ar n-a
léigean-san ar siúbal ; na gadair do léigean ar an b-fiaig.

lamenting over him ; he
rolled a stone unto the
door of the sepulchre ; they
were feeding in a meadow ;
aiming at him.
M. and A. go to Pharao ;
Patrick's visit to the clergy
of Ulster ; a hosting of Niall
and his sons to go against
the English ; when I was
glorying in you ; he excelled
(all) Ireland.

praying for you ; they upset
the house ; he lighted on
the cashel of the church ;
no one will dare to draw
your blood ; the hag has
betrayed thee.

He overthrew their tables ; to
tax a country ; he pursued
them ; not to follow (treat
of) them further ; I shall
visit their sins upon them ;
Job continued his parable.

their blood shall be required
of this generation ; his blood
pursues us, is required of
us ; to dwell on or hammer
out a thing ; she followed D.
by his track ; no one is read
of who put. . . .

he let fall a word or two ; I
dropped my watch ; to
neglect ; he postponed it ;
when he defers his amend-
ment.

give him rope enough ; to let
loose ; they shall all kneel
upon their knees ; when
they were dismissed ; to
hound the stag.

foirġníoṁ do léigion ar neiṁní
do díoth a chongbála suas;
ro léiced h-Eriu ar raind
Ameirgin; d'eagla ar d-tru-
ime do léigean ar aon neach
agaibse; níor léig mé orm
féin bur measg-sa eolas do
beith agam ar níd ar biṫ
acht aṁáin ar Iosa Criost
agus é fós ar na cheusad.

to let a building go to ruin for
want of keeping it up;
Ireland was left to Ameirgin's division, *i.e.* to be
divided by him; that we
might not be chargeable to
any of you; I have not pretended (or determined) to
know anything whatever
among you save Jesus
Christ and him crucified.

neach do léigeas aimideacht
air féin do ḋruim cleasuiġ-
eachta; léigid sé air go b-
fuil grád aige daṁsa; do
léigean galair bréige air féin.

one who pretends to be a
fool through tricks; he pretends to love me; to "let
on," pretend, to be sick.

do léimiod ar neach; ná
leum air; do leathfaide do
raḋarc ort; liim-se forru-som
díltud eissérgi Críst; líit
fornn á épert; *a.* do theampull Jerusalem ro liset-sum
for Iosa sin do ráda.

to fly at a person; do not
fight him; your sight would
be dazzled; I attribute to
them (charge them with)
the denial of Christ's resurrection; they accuse us of
saying it; they imagined
Jesus to speak of the Temple
of Jerusalem.

ro lingeadar air an ṁéid
ar a rabadar easláinteaḋa;
do ling ar bórd na luinge
an sgian sgóithgeur; an
tan do ling an pobul air
d'éisteacht ré bréithir Dé;
lingfiḋ cach ar a lorg.

as many as had diseases
pressed upon him; he flung
the sharp knife on board
the boat; when the people
pressed upon him to hear
the word of God; the rest
will pursue him.

ag lorgaireacht ar mo ġnóth-
uide; teach do loscad air;
a. ro loisced orra Luim-
nech.

prying into my affairs; to burn
a house of his; he burned
Limerick on them (*i.e. their*
city; *not* over their heads).

luaiġ ort; guidim thú luaithiġ
ort, léiġ daṁ; neach do
luathuġad ar a choiscéim-
idc; luiġe go trom ar an
neiṁchiontach.

haste you, hurry; go to, I
pray thee, let me; to mend
one's pace; to oppress the
innocent.

tan do luiġ an t-iomurcaiḋ orra dob' éigean dóib chlaonaḋ.

gach leaṫtrom dá luiġeaḋ orra ; luiġiḋ m'anam ort ; is é an tí ar a m-bí an bróg is feárr fios cá luiġeann sí air ; luiġim ar mo stuideur ; dobeirid ar an druing ar a luiġṫear cóṁairc do deunaḋ

do luiġe ar forfaire ar ní ; luiġṫhe go dian dásachtach ar ní ; do ṫromluiġ sí air ; do luiġe ar gur ar uiġe ; ag luiġeachán air ; óir cheana atáid ar luiġeachán ar m'anam.

bíd briaṫra an drochḋuine 'n-a luiġe a g-ceilg ar fuil ; mar do beiṫ mórán ag machtnaḋ ort ; gach a b-faiceann mé atáid ag magaḋ orm ; acht anois an drong is óige na mise atáid ag magaḋ orm.

tug sé Eabruiḋeach asteach do ṁagaḋ oruinn ; ṫáinig sé asteach chugam do ṁagaḋ orm ; do magaḋ ar neach ; o. do deunaḋ fonoṁaid faoi ; o. do rinne sé cloch rothnóis díomsa ; bí sé ag magaḋ fá' n eagla agus ní bí uaṁan air.

do ṁaireadar ar beagán bíd ; do ṁaoid sé orruinn go raiḃ fleaḋ aige fá chóṁair Fhinn ; do ṁarcuiġeacht ar each ; o. cách do marcuiġeacht ; meabraiġmid ar ár léiġionn ; do ṁeaṫ a mianna orra ;

when they were overpowered they were forced to give way.

every trouble that befell them ; my soul hangeth upon thee ; the wearer best knows where the shoe pinches ; I betake myself to my study ; they make the oppressed to cry.

to wait for a thing ; eagerly bent on a thing ; she overlaid it ; to hatch eggs ; lying in wait for Him ; for lo! they lie in wait for my soul.

the words of the wicked are to lie in wait for blood ; so that many were astonished at you ; all they that see me laugh me to scorn ; but now they that are younger than I have me in derision.

he hath brought in a Hebrew to mock us ; he came in unto me to mock me ; to mock him ; to mock him ; he made a mockery of me ; he mocketh at fear and is not affrighted.

they lived on little food ; he boasted to us that he had a feast for Finn ; to ride a horse ; to ride (over) others ; let us study our lesson ; "things don't go well with them" ; things did not suc-

o. ni b-fuilid na neithe ag éirġe leo.

do ṁeath dídean orm; do ṁionnuiġ orm féin; má ṁóthuiġeann sé buairead ar a choinsíos fa ní throm ar bith; ar a ḋeilb do measfaḋ tú gur duine macánta é.

ceed with them.

"periit fuga me," I had no shelter to flee to; by myself I have sworn; if he feel his conscience troubled with any weighty matter; by his looks you would take him to be an honest man.

neach ag a m-bí meas mór air féin agus gan meas ag cách air; measfuidthear 'na ṁalluġad air é; do mes for bíu ocus marbu; messimir-ni forru-som; *a.* messimir-ni forru forsan-mitter.

one who has a great opinion of himself and is not esteemed by others; it shall be counted a curse to him; to judge the living and dead; we shall judge them; we shall judge them whom thou judgest.

do hoileaḋ ar feoil naoiḋenán í; ól orm! ol deoch orm; atáim ag ól ortsa; *o.* atáim ag ól chugadsa; an té atá suas óltar deoch air, an té atá síos, buailtear cos air; ordóchaiḋ mise mé féin ar eisiomláir-sion.

she was fed on the flesh of infants; drink to me; I pledge you; I drink your health; whoso is up his health is drunk, who is down is kicked; I will regulate myself by his example.

a. do rír a einech ar chuirm; do réiġteach air; do réiġteach ar síoth; riothaid sé orm mar aitheach; do rioth ar lán luais ar neach; do rioth ar thalaṁ asteach aṁuil long buailtear a d-tír; long do rioth ar thalaṁ; go roisir ar neaṁ.

he sold his honour for beer; to agree to it; to agree to a truce; he runs at me like a giant; to run full butt at one; to run aground as a vessel which is struck against the land; to run a ship aground; may you reach heaven.

cubaid cia mad for Tomás no saided Isu sech na hapstalu archena; ro saiġ an mac coṁrad ar tús ar an athair; ro saiġsiot Danair forra; do saith sé orra, agus ar n-a g-claoi dó do

it was proper that Jesus should address himself to Thomas before the other Apostles; the son first began the conversation with the father; the Danes attacked them; he rushed on them and

buaduiġ sé orra.

ní cóir do neach sáthad asteach ar chéird duine eile; do sáthad asteach ar an b-fómós dliġeas neach do phearsanaib cáilideachta; níor saltradar coiléin an leoṁain air, agus níor ġab an leoṁan borb láiṁ ris; do sartuilt ar an b-feur.

ná teilgid bur g-clocha uaisle a b-fiadnuisi na muc, ar eagla go saiⁿteoraidís orra le n-a g-cosaib; buille do sanntuġad air; do sáruiġ air agus do ġab sé an tiodlaicead; do sáruiġ sé orra go mór; do sáruiġeadar go mor an t-óglach.

do chonnairc mé go sáruiġeann gliocas an leiṁe.

sásfuidthear m'antoil orra; tá mé sástaid air, má tá tú sástaid air; sásóchthar m' anam orra; d'eagla go scinnfidís ort.

as insgríobtha chuca iad féin do seachnad ar thruailliġthib na n-íodal agus ó ḟuil; go seachna sib sib féin air fuil agus ar neithib tachduiġe; iarraim d'athchuinge orraib sib féin do seachnad ar ainṁianaib na colna; seachnaid sib ar an t-saint.

cia d'a b-fuilim ag saothruġad agus d'a seachnaim m'anam ar ṁaith?

do seachain mo ġrád é éin.

overcame them, and prevailed against them.

it is not right for anyone to break in upon the province of another; to break in upon the respect a man owes to persons of quality; the lion's whelps have not trodden it, nor the fierce lion passed it by; to tread upon the grass.

cast not your pearls before swine, lest they trample them under their feet; to strike a blow at him; he urged him and he took the gift; he pressed, urged them greatly; they pressed sore upon the man.

I saw that wisdom excels folly.

my lust shall be satisfied upon them; I am satisfied if you are satisfied; my soul shall have its fill; lest they should spring at you.

they are to be written to, that they abstain from pollutions of idols and from blood; that ye abstain from blood and from things strangled; I beseech you to abstain from the lusts of the flesh; beware of covetousness.

for whom do I labour and bereave my soul of good?

my love had withdrawn himself.

I

do chuir sé mo ġruag 'na seasaṁ orm; is éigean duit seaṡaṁ go hiomlán airsin; do ṡeasaṁ ar ṅeithiḃ neaṁtháḃachtacha; is é ní is mó ar a seasuíġthear.

he made my hair stand on end; you must chiefly insist upon that; to insist upon trifles; this is the thing most insisted on.

seasaid ar na Francaiġ ar son gach nuadnóis eudaiġ; níor ṁaith liom do ṡeasaṁ a ḃfad ar an b-príoṁádḃar soin; seasuiġim ortsa; seasuiġid siad 'san uile ní ar ráidtib na heaġailse.

they depend upon the French for every new fashion of dress; I would not have you dwell long on that subject; I rely upon you; they depend in all things on the lips of the clergy.

doḃeuraid mé ar íasg th' aḃann seasaṁ ar do lannuiḃ; do ṡéidead ar siubal é; noch seinneas go gasda ar chláirseach; do ṡinnim ar an g-cláirsiġ; do ṡinnim ar aon teud do ġnáth; sgaoil ar siuḃal é.

I will cause the fish of your rivers to stick to your scales; to blow it away; who plays well on the harp; to play the harp; to harp always on one string; let him go.

sgoiltis a chroide ar a dó; siúbail ar ṡoillse an lae; neach do ṡeolad ar láiṁ; do seolad ar seachrán iad; do chuaid neach áiriġe chuige ag sleuchtain ar a ġlúiniḃ dó.

he severed his heart in twain; walk in the light of day; to lead one by the hand; they were led astray; there came to him a certain man kneeling down to him.

slóiġead la C. for U.; do sméideadar ar a g-cómpánachaiḃ; ar sméidead láiṁe dósan orra chum beith 'na d-tocht; beatha do ṡocruġad air ar fead a beatha.

a hosting (was made) by C. against U.; they beckoned to their partners; he beckoned unto them with the hand to hold their peace; to settle a pension on him for life.

do ṡraoil sé ar aġaid le n-a chosaiḃ agus le n-a láṁaiḃ; do streachladar é le foirneart ar cheann agus ar chluasa; ar suide dó ar an m-bórd; ar m-beith curtha agus

he crawled along on his feet and hands; they hauled him by the head and shoulders; as he sat at meat; Jesus being tired and weary with travelling sat by the

tuirseach d'Iosa ó'n aisdear, do śuid sé ar an tobar; do śuideadar ar śleasaib na bruidne do réir a n-uaisle.

do śuide ar an stiúir; do suide ar gur ar uiġe; do suidead air é; is cóir dí creidioṁ neithe do śuidead orrainn; creud as a d-tugann mé iomad rann mar śuidiuġad ar an stair.

a. do thaiscelad for ríg Erenn; do thaisdiol ar muir agus ar tír; ní con talla obbad fair itir; tarassair for a cind; do tharbaid sé orra; rob é méd an smachta agus annirt tarraid sé forraib.

adṁolad an domain uile do tharrang air; neach do tharrang ar chluais; níd do tharrang ort; do tharraing sí a cocal ar a heudan; a buaitiside do tharrang air; gach duine ag tarrang uisge ar a ṁuilleann féin.

do tharraing mé teinid air; do tharrang teined air; do theannadar-son orra; ní gnáthach go d-teipeann ar an g-claonad úrchóideach-sa; tesbanat boill airiu.

tidacht ar comairli mná; tiomáin air; tiomáin air; tiomáin ort; tocomla F. for séd; do thógadar geur-lanṁuin ar Phól; cia ar a d-tógbaid rígthe na talṁan cíos nó cánachas? an ó n-a g-cloinn féin,

well; they sat at the sides of the court according to their rank.

to sit at the helm; to hatch eggs; it was proved against him; she ought to enforce our belief of things; why do I adduce many poems as proof of the history.

to betray the king of Ireland; to travel by sea and land; he admits no refusal at all; he tarried waiting for them; it profited them; so great was the control and sway he gained over them.

to get the praise of all the world; to lug one by the ear; to nigh or approach a thing; she drew her veil over her face; to draw on his boots; every one drawing water to his own mill.

I brought fire to it; to take a shot at him; "they were the more fierce or earnest" they pressed on them; this sad proneness to sin seldom fails (to cast headlong); limbs fail them.

to come at the instigation of a woman; fall upon him; drive at it; go on; F. proceeded on his way; they raised a persecution against Paul; of whom do the kings of the earth take custom or tribute? of

nó ó choiṁthiġe ?

ag toirmeasg oruinne labairt ris na Cineadachaib chum a slánuiġthe ; do thoirmisg tú mise ar dul ar m'aġaid níos faide ; toirmisgthear orra a chéile do phósad ; ag so an réasún aṁáin do thoirmisg orm ; do toirmisgead é ar a oific agus ar a churum ; creud iad na hoibre atá toirmisgthe oruinn ?

do thoirmisg sé an ṁíchiall do bí ar an b-fáith.

toirmisg ciapáil briathar.

toirmisg ceasta éigcéillide.

sanntuiġmíd an níd bíos ar n-a thoirmeasg orruinn ; tlochtad reuma lé g-coisgthear anál ar neach, ro coisccit arthraiġe na Banna forra ; coisg do phuisínide ar bréig ; do chosg ar an b-foircheadal neaṁda so na tortha do thabairt ; cosg ort !

an lucht atâ ag tóruideacht ar m'anam cuirid paintéir roṁam ; a. do thréig cech dán ar diadacht ; iar d-tréigean a ríge ar chléircheaclit ; an né nach tusa do threoruiġ ceithre míle fear do lucht fionġoile leat ar an b-fásach ?

do ṡír sé fá g-cuairt dream éigin do threoróchad ar láiṁ é ; do treoruiġead ar an b-fásach é ; do threoruiġ sé é ar ṡliab árd ; do throid-

their own children or of strangers ?

prohibiting us to speak to the Gentiles that they may be saved (18); you detained me from proceeding any further; they are forbidden to marry one another ; here is the only reason that prevented me ; he was suspended from his office and employment; what works are forbidden us ?

he stayed the madness of the prophet.

shun babbling.

avoid foolish questions.

we desire the thing which is forbidden us ; a catarrh by which one's breath is stopped; the boats of the river Bann were forbidden them ; keep your lips from lies ; to hinder this heavenly instruction from yielding the fruits ; stop ! give up (that conduct).

they that seek my soul lay snares for me ; he forsook every profession for piety ; after resigning his kingdom for the clerical state ; art not thou that leddest out into the wilderness 4,000 men that were murderers ?

he went about seeking some one to lead him by the hand ; He was led into the wilderness ; he led Him into a high mountain ; they

eadar le chéile ar a cheann ;
tuairisg ar neithib do chuaid
thart.

quarrelled about it ; an account of past things.

agus dá n-déarnad tuitim air
i n-agra ; atá do choirthe
féin ag tuitim ort ; an oídche
do thuitim air ; *o.* do thuit
sé ar agaid chum an talman ;
tuitfid a milleun ormsa ; do
thuit a chodlad air-sean.

and if he should do it his
challenge is to be void ;
your crimes are come home
to you ; he was benighted ;
he fell forward on the
ground ; the blame of it will
light upon me ; he fell asleep.

do thuit a n-eagla orra ;
isead tuitide ar an n-
díleachta ; do thuit sé ar
láim a námad ; do thuit
smédearnach chodalta orra.

they were afraid of them ; yea,
ye overwhelm the fatherless ;
he fell into the hands of his
enemies ; they slumbered.

.

INDEX OF IRISH VERBS.

INDEX OF ENGLISH VERBS.